Jane Hall

The Experts' Guide to
FOUNDATION PIECING

15 TECHNIQUES & PROJECTS

C&T PUBLISHING

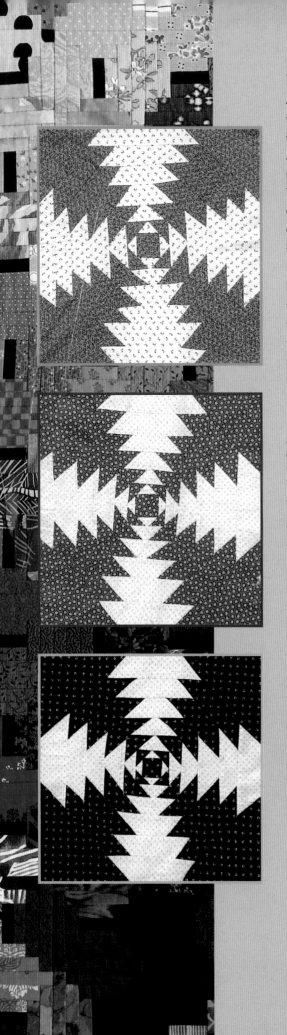

Text © 2006 Jane Hall

Artwork © 2006 C&T Publishing, Inc.

Publisher: Amy Marson

Editorial Director: Gailen Runge

Acquisitions Editor: Jan Grigsby

Editor: Deb Rowden

Technical Editors: Carolyn Aune, Ellen Pahl

Copyeditor/Proofreader: Wordfirm Inc.

Cover Designer: Christina Jarumay

Book Designer: Rose Wright

Design Director: Rose Wright

Illustrator: Wendy Mathson

Production Assistant: Kiera Lofgreen

Photography: Luke Mulks unless otherwise noted

Published by: C&T Publishing, Inc., P.O. Box 1456, Lafayette, CA 94549

Front cover: INDIGO LIGHTS, by Jane Hall

Back cover: SQUARE DANCE, by Caryl Bryer Fallert; FLORAL STARS, by Carol Doak;

LITTLE FISHES TOO, by Judy Mathieson

Library of Congress Cataloging-in-Publication Data

Hall, Jane,
  The experts' guide to foundation piecing : 15 techniques & projects / from Jane Hall.
    p. cm.
  ISBN-13: 978-1-57120-362-5 (paper trade : alk. paper)
  ISBN-10: 1-57120-362-1 (paper trade : alk. paper)
  1. Patchwork--Patterns. 2. Quilting--Patterns. I. Title.

TT835.E94 2006
746.46--dc22

2006008212
Printed in China
10 9 8 7 6 5 4 3 2 1

Contents

Preface

*There are no absolute "shoulds" or "musts" —
there are almost as many ways to work in quilting
as there are quilters working.*

This book is the result of years of teaching with other foundation piecers. Two friends who teach foundation piecing differently from the usual methods say they almost never begin a class without someone raising his or her hand and—very politely—telling them, "You are not doing it the right way." Quiltmaking allows us to be totally in charge. There are no absolute "shoulds" or "musts"—there are almost as many ways to work in quilting as there are quilters working. The operative phrase is, if it works for you, do it. There really isn't a right or a wrong way in any part of our art.

There are, to be sure, some tried-and-true methods and tips that work well. It is worth trying them to see if they work for you. There is usually a reason that they have become "tried and true." However, if you don't ever try anything new, you may miss out on a lot of interesting and creative ways to do things. When I began piecing on foundations, there were two basic ways to work, although there were many tips about different materials for foundations, different ways to mark the patterns on the foundations, and nifty tricks to help with things such as mirror imaging and cutting fabric appropriately.

In recent years, several truly different foundation-piecing techniques have emerged. This book is an effort to chronicle some of them, but it is by no means exhaustive. It is not and cannot be complete, as long as quilters are working in the medium every day. I have made no attempt to include all the patterns and ideas, nor the many wonderful designers who have fed our appetites for new foundation work over the years. The book is simply a compilation of the different ways to piece on foundations that I have come across.

This old-made-new technique has become an important component of our piecing routines. Traditional, innovative, simple, and incredibly intricate—there truly is something for everyone's taste. We are blessed with a richness and variety of designs and techniques to whet our appetites and lead us on to more wonderful quilts.

Thanks to all who have helped in this venture—colleagues, consultants, and editors. Thanks especially to families and friends, who have put up with us and encouraged us during this time.

I would like to dedicate this book to all our students, who energize and inspire us to write and teach and spread the word—and to get it right.

CHAPTER ONE

Foundation Piecing—
Past and Present

Piecing on a foundation is an old-made-new technique that has been attracting the attention of contemporary quiltmakers for several years now as they discover the benefit of stitching fabric together with a layer of *something*. Our grandmothers and their mothers knew about this. They created usable fabric from waste scraps and strips.

Today we are relearning the basics of this method of piecing. We did not invent this technique—we are taking what came before and expanding on it.

A foundation is any material used to piece *on* or *with*. It can be fabric, interfacing, paper, batting, or flannel. Foundation piecing is a technique first used in the nineteenth century to stabilize pieces of fabric stitched together. These fabrics might have been scraps, or fabrics of differing weights. Often, they were not cut on grain so they were easily stretched or distorted. When sewn onto a foundation, the resulting piece was stable and the finished size was accurate because the fabrics were controlled by the underlying base. An obvious bonus was that usable fabric was constructed out of cast-off bits and pieces.

The oldest and most common method of doing this is what we know today as *flip-and-sew*, or by its more proper name, *pressed piecing*. Pieces of fabric are stitched together on top of a foundation. The top piece is pressed open against the foundation, and more pieces are added and pressed open until the foundation is covered.

This technique was first used in this country, as far as we can determine, in the third quarter of the nineteenth century for Log Cabin and Pineapple designs, and a bit later in the century for string blocks and shapes. The foundations were almost always fabric—usually what we would call waste fabric, left over from other uses. These foundations were often quite heavy and could be of different weights in the same quilt. That may be one reason why early foundation-pieced quilts were usually tied rather than quilted. The extra layer of heavy fabric would have made the quilt extremely difficult to hand needle, which was the only method of quilting at that time.

Early Log Cabin quilt top (front)

Early Log Cabin quilt top (back)

When Dixie Haywood and I investigated the historical use of foundations for one of our books, we were surprised to find that the simpler string designs were not the ones used first. In fact, the earliest documented uses of any foundations were for Log Cabin designs, discovered in the early nineteenth century in several parts of Great Britain. The pattern was first found in the United States during the third quarter of the nineteenth century, which began the "heyday of the Log Cabin" design (*Clues in the Calico*, Barbara Brackman, EPM Publications, 1989). Early Log Cabin quilts were often made of scrap fabrics cut into strips, carefully separated into light and dark values, and pieced around a center square. Cottons and dress materials were used initially. Silks and velvets, following the trend toward "fancy work" in quilts, were used toward the end of the century.

Antique Pineapple Log Cabin quilt, detail

Antique crazy quilt piece made with fancy fabrics, embroidery, and embellishments

The Pineapple is a Log Cabin pattern gone a bit berserk. Four diagonal logs are added to the horizontal and vertical logs, making a total of eight sections. This variation didn't appear until the last quarter of the nineteenth century, but it has remained popular to this day because of its strong graphics and the many ways it can be colored.

The Victorian crazy quilts of the late nineteenth century also used foundations, usually heavy cotton squares, as bases for the overlay of lush silks and velvets of varying textures and weights. These designs were for the most part fabric collages, appliquéd rather than pieced. Patches were held in place with long basting stitches. Silk embroidery stitches held the pieces in place permanently and were worked along the seamlines as well as within larger areas of the patches. Beads, ribbons, and other embellishments were often added.

Quiltmakers in the late nineteenth century and early- to mid-twentieth century used mostly fabric foundations for Log Cabin blocks, as well as for all kinds of string designs pieced onto squares, triangles, and diamonds. As paper became more widely available, string designs were often pieced on newspaper foundations, which were sometimes left in the quilt for added warmth. This can help in dating the quilt pieces. I have a wonderful eight-pointed star pieced on colored comic pages from a 1936 Sunday newspaper.

String Star block, front   String Star block, back

When Dixie and I wrote our first foundation-piecing book, in the late 1980s, the quilt revival was in full swing and the world of quiltmaking was bursting with innovative pieced designs: rotary-cut designs, strip piecing, and new tools and books. It was a perfect time to reintroduce piecing on foundations. We both loved Pineapples. We designed and drafted them, and even created similar quilting patterns, but we foundation pieced in two different ways. In *Perfect Pineapples* (C&T Publishing, 1989), we presented our separate techniques so quilters could choose which they were most comfortable with.

TOP pressed piecing

Dixie sewed in the traditional way, stitching two pieces of fabric on a foundation. The top piece was pressed open against the foundation. The next piece was added with right sides together, stitched with a $1/4''$ seam allowance, and opened as before. This is the oldest technique for sewing on a foundation that we have been able to discover. We called it *top* pressed piecing since we were sewing on the fabric on top of the foundation.

UNDER pressed piecing—a major variation

Pineapple block on lightweight muslin

I had stumbled onto a different way of doing this a few years earlier when teaching the Pineapple block. Many quilters are not able to sew an accurate seam allowance consistently, so blocks are often not quite all the same size. I drew the pattern on a foundation (lightweight muslin or light gingham check) and pinned fabric pieces to the wrong or un-drawn-on side of the foundation. When the assembly was turned over with the fabric against the feed dogs, I discovered that even beginners could sew on the line and not have to worry about stitching with a consistent seam allowance.

The steps of opening the top piece, pressing it against the foundation, and adding the next piece were the same as the *top* pressed piecing method. The difference was that the actual stitching was done on the drawn lines of the foundation, not on the fabric. Stitching on marked lines makes all the blocks finish at exactly the same size, without relying on sewing exact $1/4''$ seams.

Other quiltmakers discovered this method at about the same time: Lesly-Claire Greenberg in Virginia, Mary Golden in New Hampshire, and Patricia Cox in Minnesota—all teachers looking for new ways to work with precision. It was truly a synchronicity, as none of us learned this method from anyone else. Dixie and I called this *under* pressed piecing, to distinguish it from *top* pressed piecing.

By the early 1990s, foundation piecing was widely accepted as a contemporary basic piecing technique. Precision was now the main advantage of using the technique. Quilters were thrilled to be able to make blocks that were all the same size, creating accurate designs with sharp points and perfectly matching intersections. *Under* pressed piecing became the most-used technique and was known by several names, including flip-and-sew, sew-and-flip, and sewing on the line. Most of the patterns were small—many were miniatures. Quilt shops sold stamps and stamped muslin squares to make Log Cabin and Pineapple blocks, as well as variations of string and crazy patch designs.

Pressed piecing has a geometric limitation: when the next piece has a cross-seam, it is not possible to continue press piecing since you cannot set in seams on a foundation. While writing a basic foundation-piecing book in 1992, and wondering why we couldn't piece a complex pattern like a Mariner's Compass on foundations, Dixie and I realized *we could piece it*. We cut a foundation into segments along the lines where pressed piecing could not continue, press pieced within those segments, then rejoined the segments using the cut edges of the foundation as guides.

Block broken into segments for foundation piecing

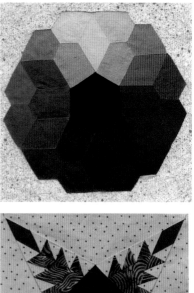

Assortment of blocks pieced on foundations in segments

We used traditional blocks to illustrate segmented foundation piecing, from the very simple to the ridiculously complicated. Some blocks used only one technique; many used a combination of two or even three, including ordinary seam-to-seam piecing. Blocks that quilters wouldn't even have considered piecing together before could now be broken into workable parts to enable difficult, even daunting designs to be foundation pieced.

Single template piecing

We also reintroduced the idea of single foundation or *template* piecing. Each patch in the block has its own paper foundation or template in this direct descendent of English paper piecing. The foundation is not sewn *on* but *with*. We consider this to be a basic technique, as the foundation is both a stitching guide and a stabilizer. This method has been used in Britain for more than two centuries for all kinds of piecing—for diamonds and squares as well as hexagons. Fabric shapes are hand basted over fairly stiff paper, and shapes hand whipped together with tiny stitches.

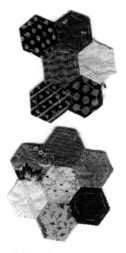

Antique hexagon piecing

The resulting piece is extremely accurate, since the quilter joins finished edges and controls the points exactly.

Today's quilters use freezer paper to make single-foundation templates. These are pressed onto fabric patches which are stitched together by machine or by hand, using the cut edges of the templates as sewing lines. As with segmented foundation piecing, the foundation is cut apart, fabric attached to each part, and the foundation reassembled into a whole. The fact that the whole foundation is fractured is more than made up for by the accuracy and control of the parts of the block when each is backed with a foundation.

In theory, any block can be pieced using *single template* piecing. However, pressed piecing is often more efficient.

Growing popularity

By the mid-1990s, many were writing and designing for foundation work. Branching out from traditional quilt genres, designers created innovative stars, original geometric designs, wonderful flowers, birds—even landscape scenes. We began to work with full-sized blocks suitable for large quilts, not just miniature quilts. Books and magazines appeared, showcasing patterns, techniques, and tips and tricks for working with this old-made-new technique.

Versatility is one of the wonderful things about working on foundations. Foundations can be used for all or part of any pattern and can be mixed with other piecing techniques. Strip piecing is easily done on foundations, trapping stretchy segments in place and adding precision, without depending solely on stitching an accurate $1/4$″ seam. Curves can be challenging with foundations, but several quiltmakers have addressed and resolved this issue neatly.

Foundations don't require templates or much measuring. Pieces can usually be rotary cut. True, it takes time to prepare the foundations, but no part of quiltmaking is without some kind of drawing, figuring, or copying. Another advantage: you can put information directly on the foundations. You can prepare an entire complicated piece, writing colors and fabric choices on the individual foundations. Construction is then a matter of matching up the appropriate fabric with the right spot, as design decisions have already been made.

New twists

With more and more quilters using foundation piecing, it wasn't long before there were patterns, books, more tips, and even more techniques available. Today, there aren't just the original two or three ways to work, but several viable and interesting new twists to this old-made-new technique. You may favor a foundation technique that is perfect for one pattern, and try an outside-the-box method better suited for another type of design. You may even have an "ah-ha" moment as you wonder why you didn't think of this first!

In the following chapters, you will meet the quilters and teachers who have developed these different ways to foundation piece. Many have been teaching and improving their foundation methods for some time. Each has provided a small project for the book, with complete instructions. Read, delight in, and explore these wonderful options.

CHAPTER TWO

The Basics—
Definitions, Technicalities, and Tips

Some techniques and tips are specific to each project in this book, but some information is basic to most foundation-piecing projects. Consider this chapter a primer on foundation techniques, to read before you begin and to refer back to as you stitch. For other basic quilting information, consult your favorite quilt instruction book.

TYPES OF FOUNDATIONS

Permanent foundations

Early foundations were almost always permanent and made from fabric. These foundations remained in the quilt, providing an extra layer of warmth as an added benefit. Before the late nineteenth century, fabric was either imported or made by hand, so it was not as readily available as it is now. Foundations were often fabric left over from garment making, and were frequently of differing weights—even in the same quilt.

When we use a permanent foundation today, we tend to use lightweight fabric or a nonwoven interfacing. Selecting the type of foundation is a conscious choice, influenced by the design, the kind of quilting and embellishment stitching planned, and the availability of a particular foundation. A wall hanging may benefit from a permanent foundation to help it hang well. If the piece is to be machine quilted, it doesn't matter that there is an extra layer inside.

Temporary foundations

Most contemporary foundation piecing is done on temporary foundations: either paper or stabilizer made of removable interfacing. These foundations are usually removed once the quilt is assembled, leaving it comparable in weight to any other pieced quilt.

A prime consideration when choosing the foundation material may be its weight, which in turn influences the stitch length for piecing. Foundation piecing does require a smaller than usual machine stitch to avoid loose stitches and distortion of the seam when the foundation is removed. On ordinary 20-pound copy paper, use a very small machine stitch (20–22 per inch, or 1.5 metric), which will remain secure even when one layer is removed. Another option: use a lighter-weight paper and a moderately smaller than usual stitch length (14–16 per inch, or 1.75–2.0 metric). Almost every contributor to this book has a preference about stitch length; the various preferences range from 12 to 22 stitches per inch. Lesly-Claire Greenberg, the "grandmother" of foundation piecing, recommends that you should never use a stitch length smaller than your seam ripper.

I prefer a 14–16 per inch stitch length, 1.75 metric. This produces a firm stitch for the seams when the foundation is removed. It is relatively easy to unsew, if necessary. The seams will be crossed by other seams, so backstitching is not needed. I begin and end stitching two stitches before and after each line. Several of the projects do not involve stitching *through* the foundation, so you can use an ordinary (12 per inch, or 2.2 metric) stitch length for the seams.

I use 12- to 16-pound tracing paper, vellum, or medical examining table paper, rather than 20-pound copy paper. Most of these are translucent, which helps when matching fabric to lines on the underside. One of my favorite foundations is lightweight inexpensive tracing paper bought in pads. It removes easily. Sometimes the more expensive art tracing paper is *too* durable and is not so easy to remove. There are many piecing papers made especially for foundation piecing, including several made by our contributors (see Resources, page 127).

Freezer paper is a popular foundation. It is lighter than copy paper and is especially useful for single-foundation templates and for designs with long skinny points such as compasses. It controls difficult, slippery, or loosely woven fabrics as well as bias cuts, but it can be hard to remove, and it is not as pliable as some other foundations. It is readily available in grocery stores in 18″-wide rolls and is also sold printed with ¼″ grids, and in die-cut 8½″ × 11″ sheets. Judy Mathieson has devised an ingenious way to fold the freezer-paper foundations and piece, which results in *not* having to deal with removing the paper in small pieces (see Chapter 5).

Several kinds of lightweight tear-away stabilizers are also available. These can be drawn on and run through computer printers. They are a little more durable than paper and, for the most part, remove easily. They are, however, more expensive than paper.

I choose my foundations based on the type and size of the quilt, the availability and cost of the foundation material, the ease of marking the foundations, and the use I plan for the quilt. A full-size Log Cabin quilt can be pieced on tracing-paper foundations, which are inexpensive, easy to mark, and tear out quickly. For teaching samples, I use Easy-Tear, a tear-away stabilizer (see Resources, page 127). It can be computer printed, is translucent, and is durable enough to be handled many times. It can also be left in the piece, and it softens after laundering, not changing the "hand" of the fabric. I definitely piece a Mariner's Compass on freezer paper—to control the points and make templates for the single-foundation parts of the design.

PREPARING FOUNDATIONS
Marking patterns on foundations

Tracing

Tracing is the oldest tried-and-true method. It is also one of the most tedious, and not without its pitfalls. It is important to offset your ruler slightly to replicate the line exactly. I use a thin ruler, not an ⅛″-thick rotary cutting ruler (which reflects overhead light and can obscure the tracing line), and a mechanical pencil for a thin and sharp line.

Tracing with a mechanical pencil and thin ruler

Photocopying

I personally don't like to photocopy patterns. A photocopy machine works in a linear fashion, from top to bottom, and it can deviate and distort the output. It may not do this all the time, but when it does it will change the measurement in one direction only. This can cause some serious problems when you try to assemble the blocks you have so carefully and precisely pieced on foundations. Copy centers can make digital copies, scanning from an original. They are a bit more expensive, but the patterns are always true.

Several of our contributors, however, use and recommend photocopying. They all stress that you should use the same machine, at the same time, and always check copies for accuracy. Barbara Barber's project requires multiple photocopies, and her technique works extremely well for a wonderfully complex design (see Chapter 4).

Computer printing

Computer printing is accurate, whether you have scanned in a design or drawn a pattern with a software program. Many lightweight foundations (tracing paper, freezer paper, interfacing) can be computer printed, although you must feed the sheets individually. Barb Vlack has become a master at using the computer to create foundations; she also uses Judy Mathieson's technique of folding freezer paper and not having to remove it in pieces (see Chapter 5).

Needlepunching

A wonderful old-timey way to replicate a pattern is to needlepunch—sewing on the lines of a pattern with no thread in the machine, top or bottom. Pin a pattern on top of a stack of up to 10 sheets of paper, set the stitch length at medium (14–16 per inch, or 1.75 metric), and sew along each line in the pattern, starting at the center.

Needlepunching a stack of foundations

The sewing machine needle punches holes in the paper, making the back side of the foundations rough, which helps hold the fabric pieces in place while you stitch. I needlepunch tracing paper, newsprint, and freezer paper. The latter is very slippery—a piece of muslin under the stack of freezer paper will help control the process.

Preset designs

There are many varieties of premarked blocks and strips, even fabric printed with piecing patterns. Stamps and stencils for small whole blocks and parts of designs are also available. As with any preset design, you must find exactly the size and shape you need.

Marking guidelines

A bonus in foundation piecing is that you can write design, color, and fabric choices directly onto the foundation. This means that the actual piecing can be almost decision-free. Lesly-Claire Greenberg was the first foundation piecer to mark numbers showing the piecing sequence on foundations. She also colors her foundations to show fabric placement (see Chapter 4).

Foundation seam allowance

If you include the seam allowance on the foundation pieces, the outside edges of the fabrics will be held firmly against the foundation. When blocks are joined, you will have more control of the positioning and pinning. The downside: after sewing, you have to tear out small strips of seam allowance foundation.

If you opt to cut out the foundation pieces on the outer seamline, you must include fabric for the seam allowance during piecing, trimming to an exact $1/4''$ after the final pressing. When you are joining blocks, the positioning and pinning will be less firm than if there were a foundation in the seam allowance, but you don't have to remove the small pieces of foundation in the seam allowance.

Depending on the pattern, I use either of these methods.

BASIC TECHNIQUES

A variety of ways to piece on foundations are presented in this book. Most are based on three primary techniques. Each can stand alone or be used with other techniques, traditional or foundation.

Top pressed piecing

The earliest foundation technique is what we call *top pressed piecing*. Its original use was to stabilize fabrics, often scraps or strips, on a base with hand stitching.

Because I enjoy the freedom of flipping and sewing without worrying about seam allowances or matching points, I use this method most often for either string or crazy piecing. Dixie Haywood pioneered non-embellished crazy quilting and has perfected the technique, creating designs with angles and texture (see Chapter 3). String piecing has long been popular, for both blocks and parts of blocks.

How it works

- Place the first piece of fabric on top of the foundation, right side up. Position the second piece on top of the first, right sides together, and stitch through all layers, using a $1/4''$ seam allowance.

- Open out the piece you just added, pressing it firmly against the foundation. Pin it down to anchor it.

- The next piece is placed against one edge of the sewn-down fabrics, right side down, and sewn as before. Trim the seam allowances either before or after stitching to reduce bulk. Repeat until the foundation is covered.

String-pieced block

String borders made with fabrics that have been used within a quilt, or with a range of tone-on-tone fabrics such as in *Indigo Lights* (page 43) in Chapter 4, provide an interesting textured frame for almost any design.

Top pressed piecing can also result in precise piecing using a measured seam allowance. Lynn Graves designed a 1/4″ sewing machine foot to ensure this (see Chapter 3). Several sewing machine companies now offer similar attachments.

Under pressed piecing

Under pressed piecing has been widely used since the early 1980s by foundation piecers who want absolute control over their stitching lines and points. Several of us began using it in the late 1970s and early 1980s, all independently of each other.

Under pressed piecing works like *top* pressed piecing; pieces are sewn together through all layers, and the top one is opened out against the foundation. The difference: once pieces are positioned and pinned in place, the foundation is turned over and the sewing is done on the foundation with the fabric *underneath*. This allows the stitcher to see and sew directly on a marked seamline.

Sewing on the line

The result is incredible accuracy with no guesswork. Carol Doak has designed paper-piecing patterns and written several books since 1993, very successfully promoting this kind of foundation piecing (see Chapter 4).

Under pressed piecing is the technique of choice for more than just traditional patterns. Eileen Sullivan uses it for her innovative designs, breaking the block into segments, and often extending the design into the

border (see Chapter 4). Peggy Martin and I both combine *under* pressed piecing with strip piecing, making the process simple as well as accurate (see Chapter 6).

Single template piecing

The third technique is *single foundation* or *template* piecing. These foundations are not sewn *on* but rather *with*. This is a direct descendent of English paper piecing, in which each patch has its own template or foundation. Instead of laboriously hand basting fabric to templates, we use freezer paper and press the shapes onto the wrong side of the fabric. Cut out the pieces, adding 1/4″ seam allowances.

Single templates pressed to fabric

Patches are then sewn together, matching the template edges. The pattern, which is drawn on paper, is reassembled with fabric attached. Foundations provide stability and accuracy, just as they do when sewn on.

Three quiltmakers featured in this book use this technique, each in a different way (see Chapter 7):

- Ruth McDowell puts the freezer-paper templates on the wrong side of the fabric in the traditional way, after drawing her pattern on freezer paper.

- Cynthia England, in contrast, feels she has more control of the fabrics and colors when she places the templates on the right side of the fabric patches.

- Caryl Bryer Fallert has used all forms of foundation piecing—*top*, *under*, and *single template*—and is now appliepiecing using single templates for curves.

Sometimes several techniques are used within the same pattern. Sheep May Safely Graze, a block from *Creature Comforts* by Barbara Brackman and Marie Shirer, was constructed with both *under* pressed piecing and *single template* piecing (see page 14).

Sheep from *Creature Comforts*

BLOCK FORMATS

Traditional foundation piecing was originally used only for whole blocks without cross-seams or set-in patches. We now realize we can break patterns into segments with more complex elements, and several projects in the book do this, joining the segments to create a block.

Anita Solomon has developed a clever way of using segmented patterns without cutting the foundations apart, which makes assembly simpler and easier (see Chapter 5).

CUTTING THE FABRIC

Shapes

A common problem of foundation piecing occurs when fabric pieces do not cover areas completely when flipped open. Pressed piecing requires a bit more fabric

than ordinary seam-to-seam piecing, probably because of being folded against the foundation. It is worth it to add that little extra seam allowance before beginning, and many of the contributors address this. This also provides wiggle room in case you have mispositioned the piece.

Regular shapes

Strips and squares are straightforward. Cut these with an *ample* $^{1}/_{4}"$ seam allowance. *Note: Make sure you do not offset the ruler, putting the edge of the fabric just inside the ruler line. This makes a scant strip width rather than the full measurement. Carpenters always allow for the depth of their saw blade—we must do the same with our fabric cutting.*

Right-angle half-square triangles can be quick-cut as usual, but using slightly larger dimensions. Instead of adding $^{7}/_{8}"$ to the leg of a triangle to get the measurement for a square that will be cut in half, add 1¼″. Make a square and cut it on the diagonal. To make quarter-square triangles, add 1¾″ to the measurement of the long side of the triangle. Make a square and cut on both diagonals. All these resulting triangles will have a ³⁄₈″ seam allowance.

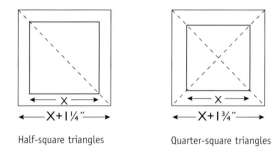

Half-square triangles   Quarter-square triangles

Irregular shapes

For shapes other than those with right angles, make a rough-cut template with a ³⁄₈″ added seam allowance as a guide for cutting fabric. This will ensure that the piece will cover the area it is supposed to, without wasting fabric. It will also allow you to control the placement of the grain of the fabric. You need only one template as a pattern from which to cut multiples.

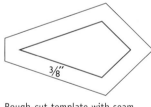

Rough-cut template with seam allowance added

We use a too-big seam allowance to ensure that the patch will cover the space adequately. But after stitching and opening the piece, it is essential to trim each seam allowance *before* positioning the next patch. Otherwise, the seam will be too deep, which will make that next patch come up short. This is true for each seam sewn, including the very first one, and most of the contributors address this.

If you are concerned about the fit of a patch, pin along the seam allowance and flip open the patch to see where it falls. With the rough-cut template and extra seam allowance, you are almost guaranteed a completely covered patch.

Marci Baker, who teaches foundation piecing, has an excellent tip for making sure that an odd-shaped piece will cover the space without wasting fabric.

● After pinning patch 1 in place on the foundation, add the fabric for patch 2, right sides together, matching the cut edges.

● Fold back the foundation on the sewing line.

● Note the shape of the folded-back area 2 on the foundation. Make certain that the patch 2 fabric extends past all the points and edges of area 2. If necessary, check the placement by stabbing pins through each corner. This allows accurate placement even with a skimpy patch of fabric since you are checking corners and edges.

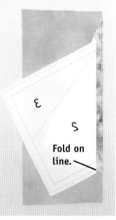
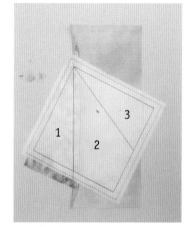

Fold back foundation on sewing line.

When line is sewn and flipped in place, fabric 2 covers patch 2.

Tip

When using odd-shaped pieces of fabric, it is incredibly easy to position them in place using the wrong edge of the patch. The simplest way to prevent this is to lay the piece you are about to attach on top of the foundation *just as it will look when it is sewn in place*, right side up. Flip that piece over, match the cut edges of the fabric, check the corners, pin it in place, and sew.

Grain line and print line

Using foundations makes it easy to control fabric direction for the shapes in a block. In general, the outside edges of a block should not be on the bias to avoid stretching. However, for the sake of fabric pattern placement, you may choose to ignore that rule since the foundation will stabilize the edges.

Mark grain/print line direction arrows on the foundation as well as on the rough-cut templates. For geometric prints such as stripes and plaids, this helps keep the integrity of the fabric design. Position points, as in the Mariner's Compass, with the grain running the long way to produce a rotating effect. Try to have the fabric grain running in the same direction on the background pieces. Even muslin has a distinctive grain, and pieces cut differently will reflect the light differently.

Mirror image

With *under* pressed piecing and *single template* piecing, you work in mirror image. Draw the pattern on one side of the foundation; position and stitch the fabric on the other side. If the pattern is symmetrical, as with a Pineapple or a Compass, it makes absolutely no difference.

If the pattern is not symmetrical—for instance, an ordinary Log Cabin block—the fabric side of the foundation will be the reverse of the drawn side. This is not a problem unless the direction of the design is important. You can counter a mirror image and have the blocks look exactly like the drawn pattern by using a translucent foundation so the lines show on both sides, placing the fabric on the *drawn* rather than on the *undrawn* side.

> **Tip**
>
> With an asymmetric pattern, mark the fabric side of foundations to make certain you always place patches correctly.

Cutting fabric for an asymmetric pattern can present a challenge. It may be necessary to cut patches individually, placing the rough-cut shape on the wrong side of the fabric so it is oriented correctly. For patterns with midline symmetry, you can cut shapes from folded fabric, producing mirror images that will fit each side.

FINISHING

Joining segments and blocks

Stab pins at the beginning, at the end, and at match points along the line. Stitch and open the two pieces to check that the lines meet exactly.

If the pieces do not match perfectly, remove stitches for about 1/2″ on either side of the offending point. Re-pin, forcing the points together, and stitch, sending the piece under the sewing machine foot from the opposite direction to the previous stitching in order to change the pressure of the presser foot.

Pressing

Press at least at the end of each row or round. Press first from the fabric side and then from the foundation side. I pin each piece after it is sewn and opened up, directly *in the seam allowance*, and it is almost as flat as if it had been ironed.

When joining segments or blocks, remove the foundations from the seam allowances and press the seams open. Pressing seams to one side is no longer as necessary, thanks to small sewing machine stitches. Seams can be pressed open to preserve points and reduce bulk.

Barb Vlack (see Chapter 5) has constructed an excellent pressing board, which is a combination of a hard surface and aluminum foil to reflect heat. It is especially suited for pressing foundation-pieced blocks and units.

Removing foundations

Restrain your urge to remove the foundations until all edges of the piece are enclosed, either by other blocks or by borders. Otherwise you circumvent one of the major reasons for using foundations—*stability*.

Using a blunt tool, such as a knitting needle, score the foundation at a stitching line, and then run the tool between the fabric and the foundation to loosen the foundation. Most of the time, the entire foundation will tear out easily. If there are pieces left, remove what comes out easily and don't fret over the tiny bits caught in a seam. They will get lost in the quilting.

Haywood

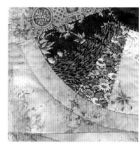

Graves

Greenberg

Doak

Hall

Barber

Sullivan

Mathieson

Vlack

Solomon

Martin

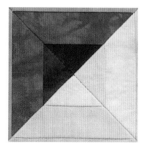

Hall

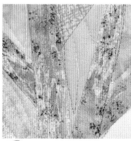

McDowell

England

Fallert

THE PROJECTS

A final word about the projects in the book: each contributor presents a project, complete with directions, diagrams, and a supply list for fabrics and other materials. In the interest of brevity, project supply lists do not include basic sewing supplies, sewing machines, and rotary cutters, unless specific tools are needed. All fabric is measured as 40˝ wide unless otherwise noted.

CHAPTER THREE

TOP
Pressed Piecing

This is the oldest recorded method of foundation piecing, and until a few years ago it was the only known method of foundation piecing. It was first used in this country in the 1860s for Log Cabin quilts, and later for Pineapples and strip-pieced designs. Today, it remains a basic and very viable foundation-piecing technique.

The technique involves placing two pieces of fabric on top of a foundation, right sides together. All layers are stitched together by hand or machine with a measured seam allowance. The top strip is opened and pressed against the foundation; another piece of fabric is positioned against the next fabric edge on the foundation, then stitched, opened, and pressed as before. Strip designs, such as Log Cabins or strings, use varied sizes and widths of fabric, flipped and sewn until the foundation is covered. Crazy patch piecing, as the name implies, uses patches or chunks of fabric, sometimes mixed with strips.

For random designs such as strings or crazies, there is no need to match precise points. The object is to cover the foundation with fabric. These quilts are often made with scraps. For patterns with sections, such as a Log Cabin, the maker strives to maintain a uniform seam allowance and strip width, so blocks end up being the same size. A square of foundation fabric is cut to size, then either pressed in half on both diagonals or marked with an × to indicate the center of the foundation and its relation to the strips as they are added.

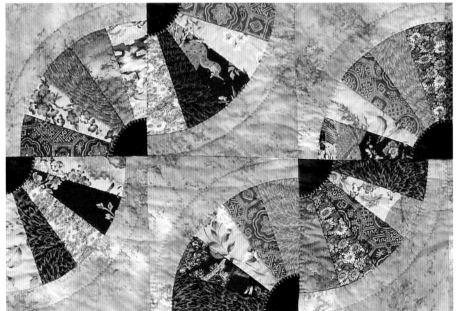

Dixie Haywood

Dixie Haywood quilts with crazy piecing designs and has written two books about her technique using top pressed piecing. She calls it non-embellished crazy patch to distinguish it from the fancy stitching of classic Victorian crazy quilting. Dixie has become a consummate designer in the genre, with works ranging from traditional designs to innovative works of art. One of her trademarks is using the same solid fabric in a block, and turning pieces so the grain of the fabric refracts light differently, as if she has used different fabrics.

Crazy piecing makes wonderful designs all by itself, but it is also an excellent technique to use for parts of blocks, or as accents mixed with other kinds of piecing or appliqué.

Dixie Haywood has been quilting steadily since the late '60s, although her first quilt was made in 1954 for her first child. A teacher, lecturer, and quilt judge, she originally received recognition for her contemporary crazy quilts but has always made all types of quilts, both pieced and appliquéd. Many of her quilts and all of her books involve foundation piecing. Dixie recently moved from Pensacola, Florida, to Pendleton, South Carolina, where she and her husband, Bob, can enjoy their daughter's family on a daily basis.

CRAZY PIECING

Crazy quilts have always been worked on top of a foundation. Originally they were a fabric collage, with each patch arranged on the foundation and secured with embel-lishment. When sewing machines came into use, many were machine press pieced with embellishment for decoration only.

When I started exploring the technique, I had no desire to replicate the Victorian extravaganzas, but rather needed to work with the varied shapes that Christmas decor, household items, and clothing often demand. I have always used cotton fabrics, rather than the silks, satins, and velvets that most associate with crazy quilts, because I like the more contemporary look they give. I use *top* pressed piecing, and originally used limited embellishment.

I found, however, that I wanted more depth than fabric alone gave. I devised a foundation of fabric with batting basted on top, which I called a blank. Piecing through that blank was a quilt-as-you-go process. Since my projects were lined, the messy back of the blank was covered. I used the same construction method with early quilts, which resulted in four layers when a backing was added. This made the quilts warm, but heavier than conventional three-layer quilts.

Blue Craze (detail) by Dixie Haywood, from the collection of Agnes Adkison, see full quilt on page 112.

By the late 1970s, I wanted lighter quilts and visible quilting. I started piecing on a temporary foundation that could be removed before quilting. As I became more interested in how the graphics of the random piecing meshed with quilting design, I turned to a non-embellished style of crazy quilting. Ironically, the earliest crazy quilt in my collection is non-embellished piecing with machine quilting, There is, indeed, nothing new under the sun.

Fabric choice formulas

I choose my fabrics carefully, coordinating colors rather than using crazy quilting as a vehicle for emptying the scrap drawer. I see non-embellished crazy quilting as a way to add texture and dimension, essentially creating fabric for shapes in the quilt or as a more interesting background for appliqué. In the process, I have come up with several different formulas. I use all of them in my quilt *Moving On*.

Same fabric: Covering the foundation with crazy quilting using only a single fabric provides the impact of a single color, with seams adding texture. This works best with a solid fabric or, as seen in the gray square, a tone-on-tone print. The angles of the piecing result in subtle shading, which can be amplified with polished, brushed, or specialty woven fabric.

Various prints, same color and value: Using prints with the same color and value, but varying scale and pattern, provides textural interest with the strong focus of one hue. Some variance is desirable as long as no single fabric pops out. This format was used in the smaller red rectangle and in the black sashing and border.

Same color, different values: This adds motion to texture as the different values lead the eye around the block. This works with all prints, all solids, or a combination of both. Higher contrast shows off elaborate cuts. Both the gray rectangle and the large red rectangle show this, using all prints.

Two-color prints: Combining a variety of fabrics with the same two colors in each fabric is a step between the previous formulas and the following one. Black-and-white fabrics are used in the bottom square and the top right rectangle. The former, with black

predominating, gives weight to the bottom of the quilt, while the predominance of white in the upper area lightens the space.

Multiple colors and values: This lively combination gives a more traditional look. It takes a little more thought, at least for me, to balance a wide variety of colors. It's helpful to piece a small sample to be sure your fabric choices work well together. This system is used in one square and in the final border, combining fabrics from the other blocks.

Moving On

By Dixie Haywood
Quilt size: 36″ × 48″

This classic example of contemporary crazy piecing uses all the different fabric choice formulas for crazy patch, each block framed with a narrow strip of fabric.

Materials

FABRIC

A variety of prints in black, red, gray, and black and white, or colors of your choice. Yardage for crazy piecing is dependent on the number of fabrics used and the size of the patches, but a total of 2–3 yards should be adequate.

- Fabric to frame blocks (contrasting color): $\frac{1}{2}$ yard
- Backing: $1\frac{1}{2}$ yards
- Batting: 40″ × 52″
- Binding: $\frac{1}{2}$ yard

OTHER SUPPLIES

- Variegated thread for machine quilting
- Foundation material of your choice (I suggest lightweight tracing paper.)

Preparing the foundations

Cut the pieces listed below from foundation material. The letters and numbers refer to the quilt assembly diagram on page 24.

BLOCKS

A – 8˝ × 16˝
B – 8˝ × 14˝
C – 8˝ × 8˝, with 2˝x 6˝ cut from 1 side (See Step 1, page 23.)
D – 8˝ × 24˝
E – 8˝ × 8˝, with 2˝ × 4˝ cut from 1 side (See Step 1, page 23.)
F – 8˝ × 12˝, with 2˝ × 6˝ cut from 1 side (See Step 1, page 23.)
G – 8˝ × 8˝

SETTING STRIPS

1 – 2˝ × 16˝	**5** – 2˝ × 12˝
2 – 2˝ × 10˝	**6** – 2˝ × 8˝
3 – 2˝ × 6˝	**7** – 2˝ × 6˝
4 – 2˝ × 14˝	**8** – 4˝ × 8˝

BORDERS

Inner borders: Cut 2 strips 2˝ × 36˝ for side borders and cut 2 strips 2˝ × 28˝ for top and bottom borders.

Outer borders: Cut 2 strips 4˝ × 40˝ for side borders and cut 2 strips 4˝ × 36˝ for top and bottom borders.

Fabric choices
Quilt body

A – Red, same values
B – Black-and-white, white predominating
C – All colors
D – Red, different values
E – Gray, same fabric
F – Gray, different values
G – Black-and-white, black predominating
Setting strips and inner border: Black, same values
Outer border: All colors

CRAZY PIECING 101

For a better understanding of the crazy piecing technique, read these steps and try a practice block before you begin to work on *Moving On.*

First patch pinned in place

1. Cut a patch proportional to the finished-size foundation. The size should neither overpower nor be diminished by the subsequent piecing. Pin in place. This is the only patch that should be precut to shape.

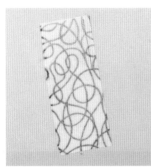

Second piece laid in place on top of first and sewn

2. Lay an uncut piece of fabric along one edge of the first patch and stitch with a ¼˝ seam allowance. Sew along the entire edge of the first patch, but not beyond it.

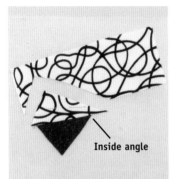

Fabric extended too far

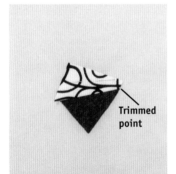

Shape cut from second piece

3. Press open and cut a shape. To avoid creating an inside angle, cut the new piece even with or back from the line that would be formed by the extension of the adjacent edges. Note the inside angle formed where the fabric extends too far. The point needs to be cut even with the edge of the center patch. Once the first patch is secured, pin the second in place.

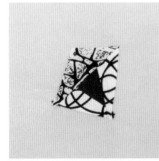

Patches added on all sides of first piece

4. Continue sewing patches, cutting to shape after each fabric piece is pressed open, taking care to avoid inside angles. Add patches evenly around the piecing to give balance and maintain proportion.

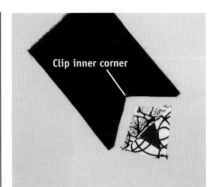

Fabric clipped to make a curve

5. To add a curve, cut an angle in the next fabric piece and clip the inner corner so it will lie flat.

6. Turn under the seam allowance, arrange in place, and press. There are 3 ways to attach a curve: (1) invisible hand or machine appliqué, which is quick and easy; (2) embellishment, when appropriate; or (3) piecing. To piece, anchor pins in the edge of the seam allowance on the fold. Carefully open the fabric and stitch along the pressed line.

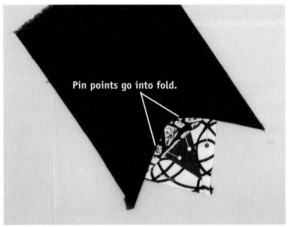

Seamline pinned for piecing the curve

7. Continue cutting shapes and piecing until the foundation is covered, with fabric extending at least ¼˝ beyond the foundation. Trim the seam allowance to ¼˝.

CRAZY PIECING 201

As piecing proceeds, especially on larger foundations, the edges formed become longer. Avoid the temptation to add fabric only partway along an edge, which will form an inside angle that cannot be pieced in a straight line.

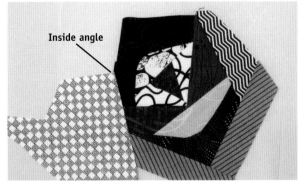

Avoid creating an inside angle

Large curves have more impact and are a good way to accent or anchor a design on a larger foundation. Cut the shape with a single curve to a position opposite the high point of the curve to accent the curve.

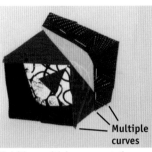

Finishing multiple curves at the same time

To cut a triple curve, pin the first curve in place as described in the basic directions. Cut 2 more curves on each side of the first, allowing for the seam allowance on either side of the space between the curves. To see how it will look, draw the angles that will become curves with chalk before you cut.

When curves are going to be closed with appliqué or embellishment, pin them in place and proceed with the piecing. When the piecing is complete, finish all curves at the same time.

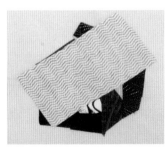

Straightening an uneven edge

If an edge is a bit out of line, stitch in a straight line and then trim the underlying piecing. This is especially important when adding lighter fabric to avoid shadow-through.

Long narrow accent strips are a way to move the eye through the piecing and bring coherence to the random shapes. Stripes can be especially effective for accent strips, either cut along or across the pattern.

Accent strips

Construction

Note: For the inner and outer borders, begin piecing in the middle of each foundation to keep the patches at either end in the same scale.

1. Mark the number or letter of the foundation on the back of each block so it won't be covered when the top is pieced. Cut away portions of C, E, and F as shown below. *Be sure blocks C, E, and F are right side up because these asymmetrical blocks are not reversible when pieced.*

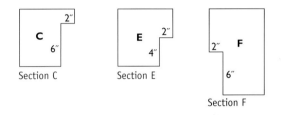

Section C   Section E   Section F

2. On the back of the block foundations, draw a line $1/2''$ from the outside edge on all edges except the cutaway sections. This will be the sewing line for the framing strips around the blocks.

3. Crazy piece the foundations using *top* pressed piecing in the colors listed on page 21, or in colors of your choice. Be sure to extend fabric beyond the foundation, and trim seams to $1/4''$ *outside* the foundation on all edges after piecing.

4. Cut 9 strips $1 1/2'' \times$ the width of the fabric for the framing strips. Cut these into pieces approximately $3''$ longer than the lengths needed to frame all sides of the sections (except for the cutaways on sections C, E, and F).

5. Using *under* pressed piecing (see page 13), sew the framing around all edges except the cutaway sections. If you use a striped fabric, miter the corners; otherwise, piece them like the borders. From the top of the block, trim the raw edge of the framing $3/4''$ from the seamline, to result in a $1/2''$ finished measurement.

6. Following the assembly diagram on page 24, construct the top into the sections listed below. *Note: Sections C, E, and F have set-in seams. To make the process easier, stabilize the inside angle on those sections by stay stitching a few stitches right at the angle, and clip the corner to the stitching. When adding sections, sew each seam from the inside angle outward.*

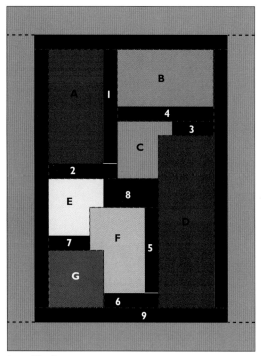

Assembly diagram

a. Add 1 & 2 to A.
   Add 3 to C.
   Add 4 to B.
   Then sew 3/C to 4/B and add 1/2/A.

b. Add 5 & 6 to F.
   Add 7 & 8 to E.
   Then set 5/6/F into the corner of 7/8/E.

c. Sew the E/F unit to the A/B/C unit.

d. Set in G and D and add borders.

7. Stay stitch around the top in the seam allowance to prevent stretching when the foundation is removed.

8. Remove foundations; layer the top with the batting and backing. Quilt as desired. My quilt was machine quilted with variegated thread in the ditch of the blocks, trim, and borders, and with a random pattern in the blocks and borders.

Lynn Graves

Another quiltmaker long associated with top pressed piecing is Lynn Graves. She is the inventive person who figured out a way to maintain an accurate seam allowance while sewing fabric pieces together on foundations. Lynn designed a ¼″ sewing foot that makes it possible to sew an exact seam allowance all the time. She has designed other tools and dozens of wonderful patterns for top pressed piecing.

Lynn Graves, of Chama, New Mexico, started her company, Little Foot, Ltd., in 1988 and produced her first product, Little Foot, in January 1989. Since introducing her top pressed piecing foundation sheets and patterns, she has taught at quilt shows, conferences, and guilds worldwide. Author of *The Frame Game*, she currently lives in the mountain country of New Mexico and has a small quilt shop as well as a worldwide mail order business.

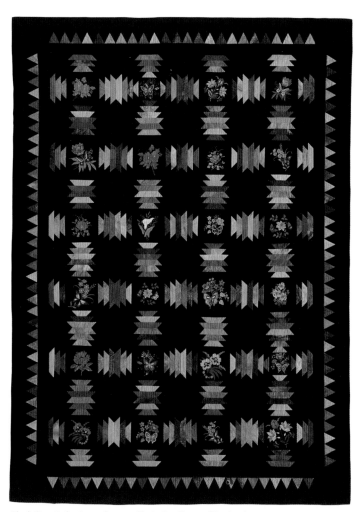

Black Beauty by Lynn Graves. Photo by Sharon Risedorph.

PRECISE TOP PRESSED PIECING

There are people for whom quilting has become a magnificent obsession. I am one of them. Quilting came into my life in early January 1985. Every quilt I saw I wanted to make. Log Cabins and all the variations stole my heart and warmed my soul. They are still my favorites today.

Because of my passion for Log Cabins, my first product was born. Our Log Cabin work-study group was making little Log Cabin blocks and mine was a tad deformed. So I went to a gunsmith and had him make an exact 1/4″ presser foot with a narrow left side so it wouldn't ride up on the previous seam allowance. I had searched everywhere for a 1/4″ foot, but there were none in 1988. Getting it manufactured was another challenge, but it was finally accomplished. It was the first of several products my company created.

It is said that necessity is the mother of invention. In 1988–89 I tried so hard to do the new method of foundation piecing—sewing on the line. Everybody was doing it. It is a wonderful method and very accurate. I saw Lesly-Claire Greenberg's rubber stamps at a quilt market and tried one, but I just couldn't get it. So I gave up and sewed the Pineapple foundation sheet with my fabric on top and my presser foot on the line. My block was smaller and my center floated, but I made a Pineapple block. I was elated!

I looked for patterns printed with fabric placement lines instead of sewing lines. When I didn't find any, I gave up and printed my own in 1990. Now designs for all kinds of patterns are available.

I have traveled the country like a gypsy for sixteen years teaching and showing my foundation sheets and tools, and I publish a newsletter, *Little Foot Press*. In 1994 I wrote and self-published *The Frame Game*, which features the Pineapple pattern as a frame for isolated motifs in the center of each block. In 1997 I was the recipient of the Fifth Annual Schmetz Golden Needle Award for my contribution to the industry. I am truly happy with my wonderful obsession with quilting.

Moo Goo Gai Fan

By Lynn Graves, hand quilted by Rita Gunter

Quilt size: 36″ × 36″
Block size: 6″ × 6″

Materials

FABRIC

- 1¼ yards total of assorted scraps for fan blades, minimum size 3½″ × 4½″
- 1¼ yards background and handle fabric
- Optional: add ¼ yard handle fabric (if different from background)
- Backing: 1¼ yards
- Batting: 40″ × 40″
- Binding: 3/8 yard

OTHER SUPPLIES

- 1/4″ presser foot
- Glue for basting (I like to use Roxanne's Glue Baste-It.)
- Nonmelting Mylar template plastic
- Foundation material of your choice for thirty-six 6″ blocks

A scrap Grandmother's Fan design pieced on *top* pressed piecing foundations.

Preparing the foundations and patterns

1. Make 36 copies of the Fan foundation pattern, (on pullout). Set the copier on the lightest possible setting that will still let you see the lines. Cut out the patterns leaving at least 1″ all around.

2. Trace the handle and background (from the foundation sheet) onto Mylar template plastic. Cut out 1 handle and 1 background. If you have enough template plastic, it is helpful to cut 2 handles and 2 backgrounds.

Cutting the fabric

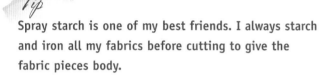

Tip

Spray starch is one of my best friends. I always starch and iron all my fabrics before cutting to give the fabric pieces body.

1. Cut a strip 3$\frac{1}{2}$″ wide from each of your assorted scraps. Subcut the strips into 3$\frac{1}{2}$″ × 4$\frac{1}{2}$″ rectangles. Each rectangle will make 2 fan blades. Cut a total of 90 rectangles to yield 180 blades.

2. Cut the background fabric into 5 strips 9″ × the width of the fabric. Each strip will yield 8 backgrounds and handles. You will need 36 backgrounds and 36 handles. (Set the strips aside for now.)

If you use a different color for the handles, cut 2 strips 2$\frac{1}{4}$″ × the width of the fabric and subcut into 2$\frac{1}{4}$″ squares. Each strip (selvedge to selvedge) will yield 18 squares.

Piecing

Please read all instructions before beginning.

The lines are *guidelines for the edge of your* $\frac{1}{4}$″ *presser foot*, not *sewing lines*. The cut edge of the fabric is placed next to the line and the side of the presser foot is placed on the line. The stitching line is $\frac{1}{4}$″ to the left of the line. The numbers on the units indicate piecing order; the arrows indicate sewing direction.

Set a short machine stitch length: 18–20 stitches per inch, or 1.5 on metric machines. Stitch from dashed line to dashed line for each fan blade.

Tip

Inside cut means trim the strip just inside the line. This line must be visible for placement. *Outside cut* means you can leave a bit of fabric over the line, as this edge will be rotary cut.

THE FAN

1. Place 2 rectangles, right sides together, on fan blade 1. Align the edge of the fabric next to the solid line separating blades 1 and 2. Begin stitching the blades at the dashed line above the solid arc. Stitch to the dashed line below the solid line of the handle. Remember, the presser foot goes on the line and your fabric is placed a tad to the left of the line.

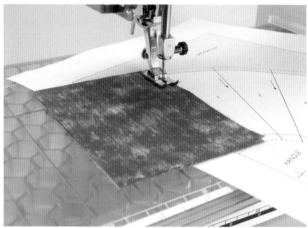

Stitching the first blades

2. Press the top piece open, over blade 2.

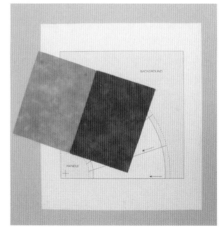

Top piece pressed open

3. Trim, using the solid line between blades 2 and 3 as a trim line. Remember, you must be able to see the line, so trim just inside the solid line (*inside cut*).

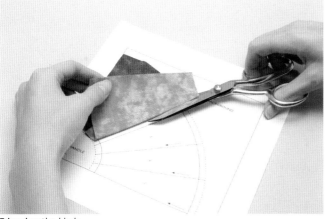

Trimming the blade

4. Trim the unsewn edge of blade piece 1 to just outside the solid line at the edge of the block (*outside cut*). Set the leftover piece aside. This piece could be used for any blade piece, but because of the angle, save it for another blade 1.

5. Continue piecing in this manner until the fan is covered with 5 blades.

THE BACKGROUND AND HANDLE

1. The templates you have made are the exact size of the background and handle. Fold one of the 9″ strips of background fabric in half, selvedge to selvedge, then in half once again. Place the templates on the fabric. If you are using the same fabric for the handles, the 2 handles will fit nicely into the melon shape between the 2 backgrounds.

Layout of Mylar templates on the fabric

2. Cut the fabric pieces an ample 1/4″ outside all the straight edges of each background and handle template. Carefully cut an even 1/4″ outside the curved arc and the curved edge of the handle. Cutting evenly around the arc is more important than the exact measurement.

3. Spray starch the arc of 1 background and place the template on the wrong side of the fabric. With a hot iron, press the 1/4″ seam allowance over the fan arc. It is not necessary to clip the curves if you have cut the seam allowance evenly.

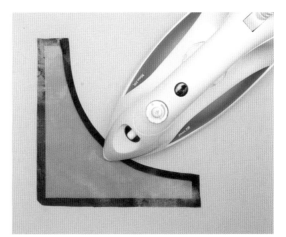

Pressing the background fabric over the template

4. Do the same for the handle. Starting to press in the middle of the arc helps ease out any little points that can form when pressing and will keep the seam allowance smooth and even.

Tip

An additional way to prevent little points and pleats from forming when pressing the arc is to begin by turning in a scant amount of the seam allowance, then push more fabric onto the template, working up to the full 1/4″ seam allowance around the arc.

Here is the magical part

Now we cheat! We are going to glue down the background and handle to hold them securely in place.

1. Place the pressed background on top of the pieced fan foundation. Where? We've covered the solid line for background placement, you say! Look at the edge of the foundation beyond the background. See the lines that extend? Simply align the pressed arc with these extended lines.

Placing the background onto the fan foundation

2. Now place a few dots of glue on the pressed-under seam allowance of the background fabric, and glue in place. Do the same for the handle, using the lines on the outer edge of the foundation sheet as guides.

Gluing the handle to the fan

3. Trim the 4 corners of the fan to expose the extended cutting lines.

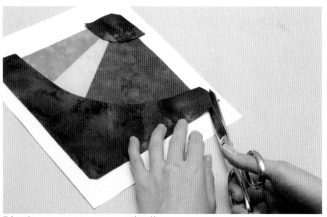

Trim the corners to expose cutting lines.

4. Trim the block using the extended cutting lines at the edge of the foundation. Align the ruler with these extended cutting lines (since we covered the trim lines with piecing earlier) and trim. The block should measure $6\frac{1}{2}$″ square.

Finishing

1. Once all the blocks are trimmed to size, topstitch the handle and the background. Use any thread or stitch you like. Sometimes you need something glitzy and fancy; other times a plain featherstitch will do. Try several different stitches in different lengths and widths.

2. Decide on the arrangement of the blocks and the size of the borders if desired. The quilt shown has 36 Fan blocks.

3. After the blocks are sewn together, remove the foundation from the seam allowances, to reduce bulk when the seams are pressed. Add borders if you have them, and then remove the foundations from the blocks.

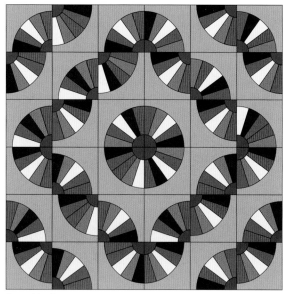

Assembly diagram

4. Sandwich the layers, quilt, and bind.

This quilt is scrap and fat-quarter friendly, but it also works well with a controlled fabric, cutting specific parts of the fabric to create secondary designs. See *Autumn Harvest*, page 113.

UNDER
Pressed Piecing

With the resurgence of interest in quiltmaking after the nation's bicentennial in the 1970s and the rediscovery of foundation piecing, it wasn't long before this old technique was reinvented.

Under pressed piecing has allowed enterprising quilters to sew on foundations *and* have absolute accuracy. Patterns are drawn on foundations, and fabric is pinned to the back or undrawn side. With the fabric under the foundation, stitching is done on the drawn line, which replicates the pattern exactly. This means that creating an exact-sized block—with perfect points and cross-seams that match—no longer depends on the quilter's ability to stitch a perfect seam. It was an amazing development, and one that led many of us to work with patterns and designs that we had never dreamed we could master with any kind of precision.

To be sure, there are new ways of working to be learned, such as mirror imaging, pretrimming seams, and allowing larger seam allowances. But overall, this foundation-piecing technique has become the most popular of all. It is variously known as flip-and-sew, sew-and-flip, and sewing on the line.

Interestingly, one of the patterns that led many of us to foundation piecing was the Log Cabin, a traditional favorite of quilters everywhere. Lynn Graves's technique evolved because she wanted to make an accurate Log Cabin. Two quilters featured in this chapter came up with even more innovations.

Lesly-Claire Greenberg

Lesly-Claire Greenberg is known as the grandmother of foundation piecing. To produce perfect Log Cabin blocks, she drew blocks on muslin, turned them over, and sewed on the lines. One of her biggest contributions was to number the logs in steps, guaranteeing that the piecing order would remain constant. In the 1980s, she created rubber stamps and paper patterns to mark foundations on fabric.

Lesly-Claire Greenberg, of Fairfax, Virginia, is an author and award-winning quiltmaker with a strong art background. She worked as an illustrator and graphic designer before she became a full-time quiltmaker in the early 1970s. Her art quilts have been exhibited at Quilt National and the Museum of American Folk Art. She designs patterns and travels to teach and lecture nationally, and she was one of the first to write a book featuring under pressed piecing in early 1993.

SEWING ON THE LINE

My work with foundations began in the 1970s. It started with some Log Cabin blocks that I just could not manage to get right. They came out curved and crooked. Those were the days of hand piecing—cutting each piece separately with shears after hand tracing sewing lines.

Many things came together to create those first individual foundations. I was familiar with foundations under crazy patch blocks and behind antique Log Cabin and Pineapple quilts.

I designed a vest pattern to sell and to be the basis of my classes. To give every student an equal chance of success, I created a muslin foundation. All the pattern placement lines were traced on it. After setting pieced blocks in place, I sewed strips surrounding them, piecing until the muslin foundation was covered. Turning back to the Log Cabin block, I tried constructing it on a foundation with placement lines marked like the vest. Surely if I placed strips on a line drawn on a foundation my blocks would be straight. The results were precise!

In the meantime, I was invited to participate in the first Fairfield fashion show. I took what I had developed for the Log Cabin quilt and launched into a Mariner's Compass cape. I drafted one section and traced it umpteen times onto muslin. Putting batting on the unmarked side, then fabric, I turned the whole thing over, *sewing on the line* to piece and quilt at the same time.

After teaching this new technique, I was ready to finish my Log Cabin quilt. I drafted a $3^{1}/_{2}''$ block using $^{1}/_{2}''$ logs and seven equal divisions. When I began making multiple blocks, I ran into trouble keeping them all turning the same direction. So I put the numbers on the foundation to follow for the piecing order.

Flower Drum Song (detail) by Lesly-Claire Greenberg. Photo by Brenda Clements Jones, see full quilt on page 114.

I showed the technique to a few friends, and my repertoire of classes increased. However, tracing foundations was a slow process. One student brought her husband along just to trace foundations! That's what prompted me to find other ways to get the image onto the foundation.

I nixed the idea of producing fabric; prewashing would distort the foundations. Next, I thought of rubber stamps. It took some time and money to hit on the right combination of rubber and ink, but once I did, I could come to class with the blocks stamped on muslin and ready to go. I made more designs and kits, and sold rubber stamps to quilt shops. Word of this new technique began to spread.

For more than twelve years, I continued making foundations on muslin. I tried tear-away, burn-away, and wash-away products but was not terribly happy with the results from any of them. In the meantime, other foundation businesses came into being, and when someone printed with my rubber stamps on paper in the early '90s, paper piecing was born.

Along came computers, with drawing and drafting programs. Now anyone could draft his or her own blocks and easily print them in any size. This created a rush to market by a myriad of home-based businesses selling foundation papers. My book, *Sewing on the Line*, was closely followed by Carol Doak's *Easy Paper Piecing*. The rest is history.

Secret Garden

By Lesly-Claire Greenberg

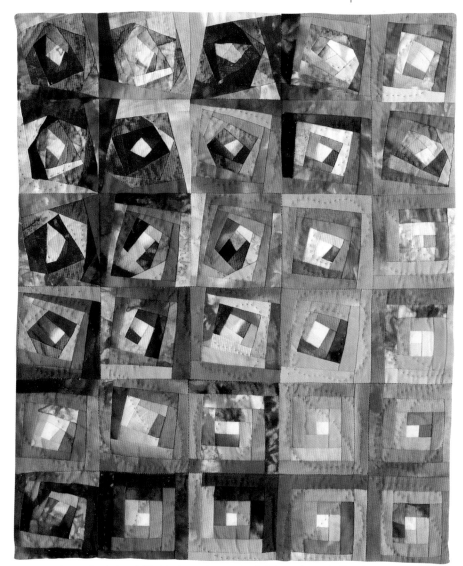

Secret Garden. A classic Log Cabin block morphs seamlessly into an improvisational rose.

Quilt size: 17 ½˝ × 21˝
Block size: 3 ½˝ × 3 ½˝

Materials

FABRIC

Select a variety of fabrics in your choice of color. The main color in my quilt is green, with accents of yellow, pink, red, and violet. The majority of my fabrics are hand-dyed or mottled in texture; all are 100% cotton. In this quilt, there is no "right" placement of color. I experimented with the placement of the light and dark values. Have fun!

- Green: assorted scraps totaling approximately 1 yard
- Pink: assorted scraps totaling approximately ⅛ yard
- Fuschia: assorted scraps totaling approximately ⅛ yard
- Purple: assorted scraps totaling approximately ⅛ yard
- Yellow: assorted scraps totaling approximately ⅛ yard
- Backing: ⅝ yard
- Batting: 22˝ × 25˝

OTHER SUPPLIES

- Foundation material (I used translucent vellum foundations; see Resources.)
- Add-a-Quarter ruler
- Postcard
- Stiletto
- Plastic-coated paper clips
- Wash-out glue stick
- $1/4''$ presser foot for final joining seams
- Long straight pins
- Optional (but helpful): Presser foot with a centerline

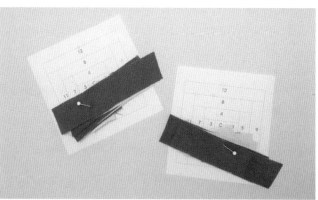

Kits of precut strips ready to sew

Preparing the foundations

1. Trace or copy the foundations on page 35. Cut out the foundations, adding at least a $1/2''$ seam allowance beyond all sides.

2. Remember when you are planning your color placement that the finished block is the mirror image of the printed foundation. I often use colored pencils to sketch in the color placement directly on the foundations. I mark off completed pieces to keep my place, particularly when I am working with a complex design.

Cutting the fabric

1. I prefer to work from strips with at least 1 straight edge to facilitate fabric placement. For Block 1, use $1''$ strips to allow $1/2''$ for seam allowances. For the other blocks, cut strips in a variety of widths, from $1''$ to $2^1/2''$, from all fabrics. You will use strips that are at least $1/2''$ wider than the sections of the block they will cover.

2. Lay the strips out on the cutting table so you can easily access them in any order. Treat the strips as if they were paint, picking them up one at a time and auditioning placement. Choose a strip the width and color needed for each section of the block, and cut it to the approximate length required. Make kits for each foundation. This way you can sew several blocks at one time, chain piecing to increase productivity.

3. Layer the precut strips, starting with the highest number at the bottom of the stack and going to the lowest number, including the foundation. Put a long pin through each stack of precut strips.

Piecing

Before you begin, remember that there are 3 simple rules:

1. All the lines are sewing lines. (*Note: There is no seam allowance added around my foundations.*)

2. All fabric is placed on the unprinted side of the foundation.

3. If you have to trim for placement of the next set of strips, fold the foundation back on the *next* line you are going to sew and trim, leaving an adequate seam allowance. I fold the foundation over a crisp postcard and trim with a rotary cutter, using an Add-a-Quarter or Add-an-Eighth ruler, depending on the size of the block.

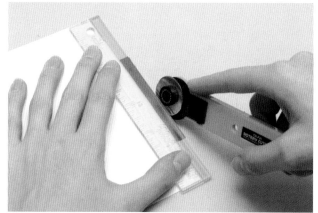

Trimming for placement of next strips using an Add-a-Quarter ruler

In a traditional Log Cabin block, there are 3 rounds of 4 strips each. When working on a Log Cabin, I work a full round before I trim. When making other configurations, I stop and trim when I can no longer easily see the trimmed edge for placement.

Tip

Before trimming, use a stiletto or a seam ripper to liberate the foundation by pushing the stitches that extend beyond the lines through the paper. *Do not pull* the foundation to free the stitches. Pulling loosens the stitches.

Using a stiletto to free up the foundation

BLOCK 1 (TRADITIONAL LOG CABIN)

The numbers referred to in these step-by-step instructions are the numbers printed on the foundations.

Center square in position and trimmed

First strip sewn and pressed

1. Always trim the center piece C to the correct size before placing the first strip. Anchor the center onto the unprinted side of the foundation with a *small* dot of glue.

2. Place strip 1 right sides together on the center piece C. Turn the foundation over, holding the strip in place, and sew on the line between the center and the first strip, aligning the drawn line with the center-line on the presser

foot. Sew a few stitches beyond the intersecting lines. Open out the strip just sewn and press it flat against the foundation. It should cover the entire designated space on the foundation with an adequate seam allowance into the adjacent areas. Finger-press, using your fingernail or the shaped wooden tool made for this purpose, pressing the strip flat against the foundation.

3. Use an Add-a-Quarter ruler to trim (see Step 3, page 32). Line up the next strip, turn the foundation over, stitch on the line, open it out, and press it flat as before.

Second strip sewn and pressed

4. Add the next 2 strips to complete the first round, lining up the long edges as before. When positioning a strip, line up 1 end of it with the trimmed edge and begin stitching at the end closest to the next highest number, letting the extra length extend over the previous strip. Trim the excess ends of the previous strips after stitching, to reduce bulk before you press the strip into its final position.

Trimming end of previous strip

End of first round, trimmed

5. Fold back the foundation on all 4 sides, 1 at a time, and trim all 4 strips for placement of the next round (strips 5, 6, 7, and 8).

Uneven Log Cabin round

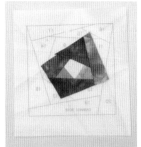

Uneven Log Cabin round, trimmed

Finished block

6. Add the next round and trim after strip 8 in the same manner as in Step 4, counting the strips to stay in order. Add the last round, and after strip 12 trim the finished block, both foundation and fabric, maintaining a $1/4''$ seam allowance beyond the outside line. Your block will measure $4'' \times 4''$.

Tip: Pitfalls

Here are some classic mistakes:

- **Feeding the strip and foundation under the needle with the fabric folded on itself (Check that the strip is flat just as you put it under the presser foot.)**

- **Trimming off the fabric you just finished sewing on**

- **Not leaving enough fabric for seam allowances at the ends of a strip**

REMAINING BLOCKS

Piece the remaining blocks as you did for Block 1, with the differences in trimming as noted below. You may trim as often as you feel necessary, but no less than suggested for a well-constructed block.

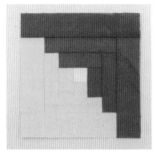

Block 2

Place strip #1; trim. Add the next round of strips and trim after #5. Continue, trimming after #9 and #13. After #15, trim the block.

Finishing

1. Lay out the blocks following the assembly diagram. Sew the short rows first.

Block 3

Place strip #1; trim. Add the next round of strips and trim after #4. Continue, trimming after #9 and #14. After #18, trim the block.

Block 4

Place strip #1; trim. Add the next round of strips and trim after #5. Continue, trimming after #8, #12, and #15. After #20, trim the block.

Make a total of 30 blocks. For this quilt, I made 9 of Block 1, 9 of Block 2, 6 of Block 3, and 6 of Block 4. Color placement on each block is unique.

2. Line up adjacent blocks with pins in the corners. Do not weave the pin—just stick it straight through the corners of the 2 blocks. Fasten the 2 blocks together with plastic-coated paper clips.

3. Sew on the line, using a $\frac{1}{4}''$ foot rather than a standard foot. The $\frac{1}{4}''$ foot will fit exactly on the outer seam allowance so it will not slide off as you are sewing the joining seam.

4. Press the seam allowances to one side, alternating the direction of the seam allowances for adjacent rows. Remove the paper seam allowances.

5. Join the rows, lining up the blocks with pins and locking the opposing seam allowances. Fasten with paper clips and stitch. If the quilt is bulky, you may choose to press these seam allowances open.

6. Carefully remove the paper foundation when the top is completed. Layer with batting and backing, quilt, and bind or face the edges of the quilt.

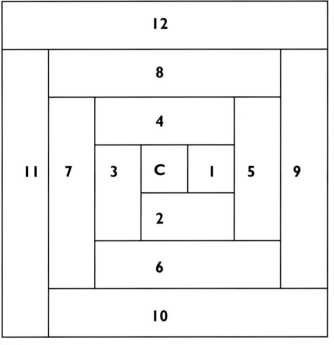

Block 1

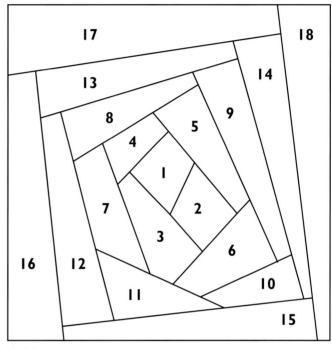

Block 3

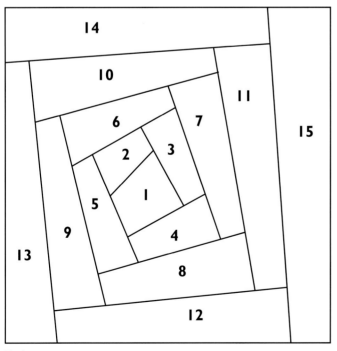

Block 2

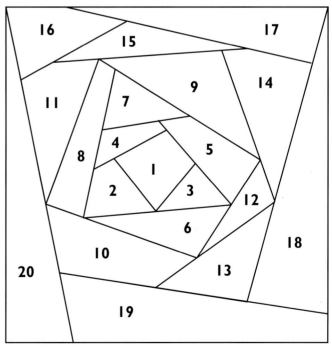

Block 4

Carol Doak

Once the technique of sewing on the line was discovered and quilters became aware of its potential for very precise piecing, it was readily accepted. When Carol Doak's first book of foundation-pieced patterns was published in 1993, she helped set the stage for an enormous surge in popularity for foundation piecing. Carol not only popularized the technique, she added tips such as using a card to simplify trimming excess fabric on top of a foundation.

Carol Doak, from Windham, New Hampshire, is a best-selling author, teacher, and lecturer. With nearly a million books in print, she has greatly influenced the art and craft of quilt-making. Her book *Easy Machine Paper Piecing* was named by *Quilter's Newsletter Magazine* in 1999 as one of the 30 most influential quilt books in the past 30 years.

Star-Crossed (detail) by Carol Doak, see full quilt on page 115.

PAPER FOUNDATION PIECING

My approach to paper foundation piecing comes from the perspective of a designer and teacher. As a designer, I often create blocks containing points to take advantage of the accuracy of foundation piecing. As a teacher, I develop an organized and uniform approach that makes it easy for a beginner to achieve success.

This approach begins with a cutting list providing the number of fabric pieces needed, the appropriate cut size, and the location where they will be used. These precut labeled fabric pieces make the process efficient and uniform.

Although you can create the foundations by tracing the pattern onto a translucent material, I prefer to print the foundations from the computer because it is quick, easy, and accurate. You can draw patterns yourself or find them on computer programs (see Resources).

The "card trick" that I developed is the method of folding the foundation over a postcard placed on the next sewing line. The fabric edge is pretrimmed $1/4''$ parallel to the seamline using an Add-a-Quarter ruler. The Add-an-Eighth ruler is used when paper piecing miniature blocks. The next fabric piece is placed right sides together along this pretrimmed fabric edge. This technique not only assists in placing the fabric pieces in a uniform way, but also allows the greatest amount of the fabric to go to the area it should fill.

Once the blocks are complete, my basting method is used to secure the beginning, the middle or any matching points, and the end. This method provides the opportunity to check for a good match, make any adjustment if needed, and easily remove the basting stitch. It also ensures that the matched points will remain secure when the blocks are joined with a regular stitch.

After the borders have been added, the paper is removed. The technique of folding on the next seamline with the "card trick" weakens the foundation at the seamlines so the paper is easier to remove.

Floral Stars

By Carol Doak, machine quilted by Kathryn Blais

Quilt size: 35″ × 35″
Block size: 5″ × 5″

Materials

FABRIC

- Dark green: $^7/_8$ yard for outer border, binding, and blocks
- Floral print: $^7/_8$ yard for inner border
- Gold: $^1/_8$ yard
- Light purple: $^1/_4$ yard
- Dark purple: $^1/_4$ yard
- Light green: $^1/_4$ yard
- Medium green: $^3/_8$ yard

- Beige: $^7/_8$ yard
- Backing: $1^1/_8$ yards
- Batting: 39″ × 39″

OTHER SUPPLIES

- Carol Doak's Foundation Paper (see Resources)
- Add-a-Quarter ruler
- Postcard or 3″ × 5″ card
- Straight pins with flat heads
- Open-toe presser foot for sewing machine
- Large (size 90) sewing machine needles
- 6″ × 6″ and 6″ × 12″ rotary rulers

Preparing the foundations

Make 20 copies of the Floral Stars foundation pattern on page 41. Space them at least $^1/_2$″ apart. If you use a copy machine to reproduce the block designs, make all your copies on the same copy machine from the original and check for accuracy. Trim the paper foundations $^1/_2$″ from the outside solid line and $^1/_4$″ outside the dashed line.

Cutting the fabric

Cut across the width of the fabric, selvedge to selvedge.

CUTTING FOR BORDERS AND BINDING

Note: The ▱ in the cutting list indicates that a square should be cut that size, then cut in half diagonally to produce 2 half-square triangles.

Floral Stars. This quilt features a block design of those wonderful points in a medallion setting that produces a central star.

FABRIC	NO. TO CUT	SIZE TO CUT	LOCATION
Dark green	2	3″ × 30 ½″	Side outer border
	2	3″ × 35 ½″	Top and bottom outer border
	4	2 ¼″ × 40″	Binding
Floral print	4	5 ½″ × 20 ½″	Inner border

Cut the following pieces and label each group with its location.

CUTTING FOR BLOCKS

FABRIC	NO. TO CUT	SIZE TO CUT	LOCATION
Gold	20	1 ½″ × 1 ½″	1
Light purple	20	1 ½″ × 2 ¼″	5
Dark purple	20	2 ¼″ × 4″	6
Dark green	10	3″ × 3″ ◹	13
Light green	20	2 ¼″ × 4″	9
Medium green	20	2 ¼″ × 5 ¾″	10
Beige	10	3″ × 3″ ◹	4
	80	2 ¼″ × 4″	7, 8, 11, 12
	20	2″ × 2″ ◹	2, 3

Sewing machine setup

- Use a 90/14 sewing machine needle. This makes a bigger hole, making the paper easier to remove.

- Use a neutral color thread.

- Use an open-toe presser foot so you can see the needle follow the line.

- Use 18 to 20 stitches per inch (1.5mm).

Tip

To speed up the process, assembly-line sew the 20 blocks.

Piecing

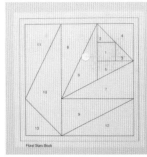

Place fabric right side up on the blank side of the paper.

1. Place the fabric 1 piece right side up on the blank side of the paper over the #1 area. Make sure the fabric extends at least ¼″ on all sides. Pin in place. Place pin away from and parallel to the #1/#2 seamline.

2. Place the card on the seamline between #1 and #2. Fold the paper back, exposing the excess fabric.

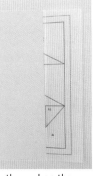 

Place the card on the #1/#2 seamline.

Fold the paper back over the card.

3. Place the Add-a-Quarter ruler on the fold and trim the extending fabric ¼″ from the seamline.

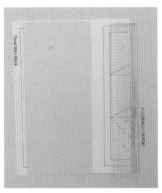

Trimming the excess fabric with an Add-a-Quarter ruler on the fold

4. Place the fabric 2 piece right side up over the area it needs to cover to correctly orient the fabric. Flip it right sides together with fabric 1.

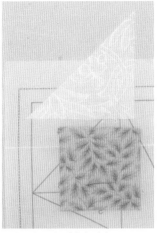 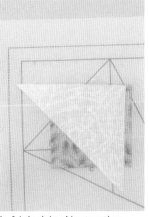

Positioning the fabric right side up

Flip fabric right sides together.

5. Turn the foundation over and sew on the seamline between #1 and #2. Start sewing about $1/2''$ before the line and extend the stitching line $1/2''$ beyond the end.

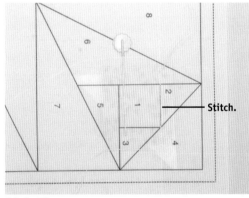

Stitched line

6. Clip the threads and press piece 2 open.

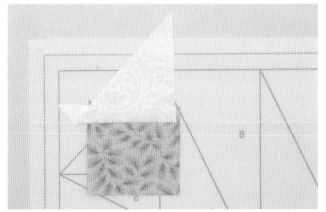

Piece 2 pressed open

7. Continue in the same fashion by placing the card on the next seamline you will sew, the #1/#3 seamline, and folding the paper back. You will need to pull the stitching away from the foundation to do this, and that is OK. Trim the fabric $1/4''$ beyond the fold using the Add-a-Quarter ruler.

Trimming for piece 3

8. Place the fabric 3 piece right side up over the area it needs to cover to check that it is the right size, flip it right sides together with the just-trimmed edge, turn the foundation over, and sew on the line between #1 and #3. Clip the threads and press piece 3 open.

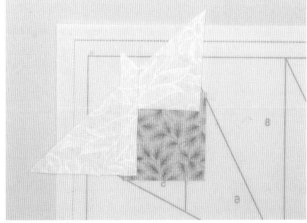

Piece 3 pressed open

9. Continue in the same fashion until all the pieces have been sewn in sequence. Using a rotary cutter, trim the completed foundation on the dashed line ($1/4''$ from the outside solid line).

Open and check for a good match.

Machine basting technique

Now that you have paper pieced perfect blocks, using this machine basting technique will ensure that your blocks will go together perfectly.

1. Place 2 trimmed blocks right sides together. Pin the blocks together, slightly away from the seamline, at the beginning, the end, and at any matching points on the seamline or at least every 3″. Increase the stitch length to 8 stitches per inch and machine baste on the seamline about 1″ at each pinned location. Do not cut the threads; just move to the next location.

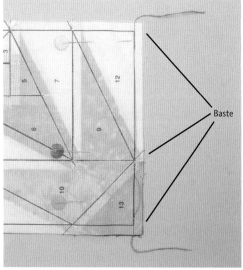

Blocks pinned for basting

2. Open the basted blocks and check for a good match. If you are pleased with the match, sew the seamline (using 18–20 stitches per inch, or 1.5–1.8 metric). If you are not pleased with the match, clip the threads on each side of the location to be adjusted and pull the thread out from the bobbin side. Readjust and baste that location again before sewing with the smaller stitch. From the fabric side, press both seam allowances to 1 side of the block.

Assembling the quilt and finishing

1. Arrange the blocks into rows, stitch, and press the seam allowances in opposing directions. Sew the rows together. Press.

2. Add the corner blocks and inner and outer borders and sew. Press.

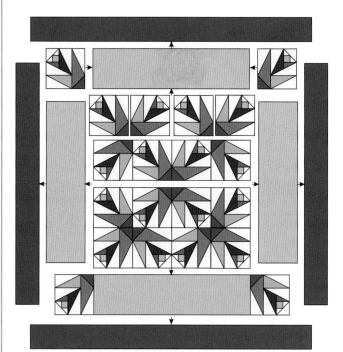

Assembly diagram

3. Starting at the outside edge of the quilt, tug diagonally on each block to pull the paper away from the stitching. Use a pair of tweezers to pull the paper from the underside of each seam allowance.

4. Layer, baste, and quilt as desired.

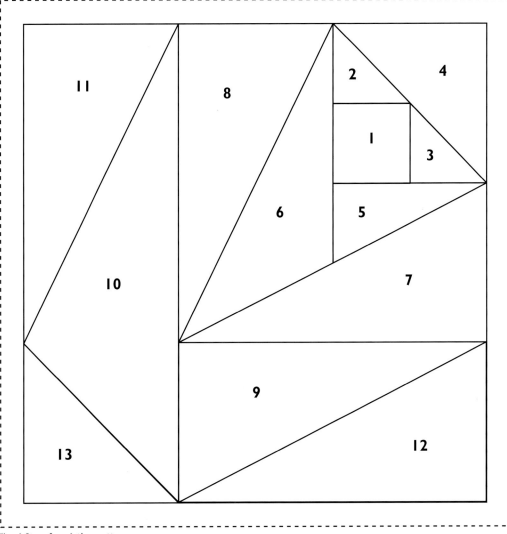

Floral Stars foundation pattern

Jane Hall

Dixie Haywood and I wrote *Perfect Pineapples* in 1989 and began a life-long addiction to the pattern. I have found that there always seems to be a new idea or a new design just waiting to be made—or, in this case, a newly found old design.

LOG CABIN/PINEAPPLE

Log Cabin and Pineapple designs are beloved around the world. In the past, they were often made using scraps and strips left over from household sewing. The Pineapple is actually a Log Cabin variation with eight planes instead of the usual four. Both have a center square surrounded by strips of fabric chosen to create areas of color or value. Both depend on contrast between dark and light values for their success as a design.

In this country, we think of the Log Cabin as typically American, depicting the journey West, clearing land, and building log cabin homes. Indeed, the heyday of the pattern was the last part of the nineteenth century. I remember being taught that the center is always red, signifying the hearth, with the logs placed to create diagonal spans of light and dark values for the sunny and shady sides of the house. It makes a wonderful and pleasing story.

However, the pattern was found in Great Britain in the very early nineteenth century. The quilters on the Isle of Man also claim its origin as theirs. It is common in Canada, and was used in the Scandinavian countries at different times in the nineteenth century. The design, with strips of light and dark values, has been found on cat mummies that can be seen in the British Museum today. Considering that the great excavations of the Egyptian

tombs took place in the early 1800s, this may account for the design's appearance in Europe in that century. As it is translated into fabric and becomes a quilt pattern, we follow in the traditional footsteps of artists everywhere, adapting shapes and colors from one medium to another.

Indigo Lights, a Log Cabin/Pineapple design, was inspired by the Ella Holcombe *Starburst* silk quilt in the Shelburne Museum. It is a marvelous design, made of blocks that are half–Log Cabin and half-Pineapple. One pair of opposite diagonal corners is the standard Log Cabin pattern, with strips overlapping. The other set of corners has the classic diagonal Pineapple strip laid across the horizontal/vertical strips. Either pattern is graphic when multiple blocks are joined, but when both are combined, wonderful balls of color emerge in the midst of the usual X design of the pieced Pineapple block.

For *Indigo Lights*, I chose to follow the proportions of the original block with a large center, making the Pineapple figure proportionate to the ball of color created by the Log Cabin corners. Any Log Cabin or Pineapple is easy to modify, beginning with the size of the center square and ending with as many strips out as you wish. Older patterns usually had more rather than fewer strips, giving a gentle stair step of color gradations.

Nebula (detail) by Jane Hall. Photo courtesy of American Quilter's Society, see full quilt on page 116. Photo by Charles R. Lynch.

Indigo Lights

By Jane Hall

Quilt size: 44″ × 44″
Block size: 6″ × 6″

Materials

FABRIC

Note: The Pineapples were made from 2 different dark blues, one print for the centers and a mottled bright navy for the strips and corners. I used varied shades of creams and beiges for half the Log Cabin parts, and different mixed batiks for the other half. The entire piece could be made with one color for all the Pineapples and another for the Log Cabins, or 1 light fabric for half the Log Cabins and 1 medium/dark for the remaining Log Cabin halves.

- Light Log Cabin areas and outer string borders: approximately 1½ yards total, same or varying fabrics
- Dark Log Cabin areas: approximately 1 yard total, same or varying fabrics
- Pineapples and inner border: approximately 1⅜ yards indigo blue
- Centers and inner border: approximately ⅜ yard light indigo print
- Backing: 1⅜ yards
- Batting: 48″ × 48″
- Binding: ½ yard

OTHER SUPPLIES
- Foundation material of your choice
- Triangle ruler for corners

Preparing the foundations

1. Trace the block pattern on page 47 and use it as a guide for needlepunching or tracing 36 foundations (page 47). For this block, I like the stability of having foundations in the outer seam allowances, so I cut out the foundation ¼″ beyond the outer lines.

Indigo Lights. This graphic quilt is made with a combination of Log Cabin and Pineapple designs within the same block.

2. Using the quilt photo (above) and assembly diagram (page 47) as your guides, number the blocks 1–36 and plan the color placement. Write the colors directly onto the foundations, remembering that the fabric will be placed on the rough side of the needlepunched papers.

Cutting the fabric

LOG CABIN AND PINEAPPLE SECTIONS
- Light fabric: Cut 26 strips 1″ × the width of the fabric for the Log Cabin sections and border.
- Dark fabric: Cut 21 strips 1″ × the width of the fabric for the Log Cabin sections.
- Indigo blue fabric: Cut 30 strips 1″ × the width of the fabric for the Pineapple sections.

Lay fabric strips against the pattern to roughly precut logs of fabric for the entire block. It is easiest to measure and cut the strips in each section at one time, adding at least a $1/2''$ seam allowance to the end of each log. Within each row or round, there will be 2 light strips, the same or different fabrics, one $1/2''$ longer than the other; 2 dark strips, the same or different fabrics, one $1/2''$ longer than the other; and 2 Pineapple strips, the same size. There are 4 complete rounds in each block, each containing 6 logs, so you will have piles of lights, darks, and diagonals, graded in size.

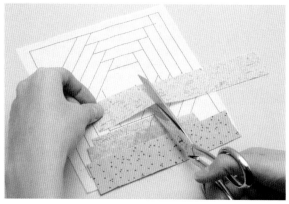

Cutting logs of fabric for one section

CENTERS

● Light indigo print: Cut 3 strips $2^1/2'' \times$ the width of the fabric and subcut into 36 squares $2^1/2'' \times 2^1/2''$.

CORNERS

● Indigo blue fabric: Cut 4 strips $2^1/2'' \times$ the width of the fabric for the Pineapple corners.

Cut 2 Pineapple corner triangles, positioning the triangle ruler evenly on the cut strip. Cutting triangles on a wide strip rather than from squares cut on the diagonal keeps the integrity of the grain line throughout the block.

Layout for cutting corners

Piecing

The Log Cabin pattern is pieced with strips sewn in sequence around the center square, creating 4 sections of fabric in the finished block. In one round, often the same value fabric is used for adjacent strips, producing

2 identical sections of each fabric. In this quilt, a different fabric was used in each section, resulting in a wider variety of fabrics and a more interesting combination of colors.

Because this is a combination pattern, instead of 4 Log Cabin strips or 8 Pineapple strips in each round, there are 6 strips. The Log Cabin strips will overlap in 2 opposite corners as in a typical Log Cabin pattern, and the remaining 2 corners will have a space that will be filled by the diagonal strip, like a Pineapple design. You will have 2 light Log Cabin strips, 2 dark Log Cabin strips, and 2 Pineapple strips. It is easy to pin and stitch 2 opposite strips at a time. Remember, you will have a light opposite a dark for the Log Cabin steps to create the specific balls of color. See assembly diagram, page 47.

1. Pin a square of fabric over the center square on the rough needlepunched side of a foundation, right side up. The cut edges should overlap the sewing lines for the center by $1/4''$ on all sides.

Center square pinned in place on foundation

2. Pin the first *short* light strip onto the center on the line between the center and space 1, right sides together, matching the cut edges. Pin the first *short* dark strip onto the opposite side of the center, on the space 3 line, right sides together.

First strips pinned in place

3. Turn the foundation over and stitch on the first line where a strip is pinned, beginning and ending with 2 stitches before and after each end of the line. Hop across to the second line and stitch. Trim threads and any excess seam allowances. Turn the foundation so the fabric side is up, open the strips, and press them firmly against the foundation. Pin in place.

First set of strips sewn and pinned open

Tip:

Keep the pins in place until the strips are anchored by the next round to keep the strips flat and prevent them from flopping over. I use only 2 pins, removing them with each new set of strips. Pin directly in the seam allowance, which is as effective in flattening the strip as ironing it.

4. Pin the first *long* light strip in place to cover space 2, right sides together, matching the cut edges. Pin the first *long* dark strip to cover space 4, on the opposite side of the center square.

Second set of strips pinned in place

5. Stitch as before, hopping from 1 line to the other. Trim the threads and excess fabric after stitching. With this size block, I like to trim the seam allowance to a *scant* $1/4''$.

6. Press the strips open and pin in place as before.

Second strips sewn and pinned open

7. Lay the 2 diagonal Pineapple strips 5 and 6 across the 2 open corners. At this point, you may opt to fold the foundation on the first diagonal line and trim the excess fabric to the $1/4''$ seam allowance from the Log Cabin strips to provide an accurate fabric placement edge for the next logs.

When I work with a pattern with guidelines of straight parallel lines visible ahead, I often save time and position the new strip by simply gauging its distance from the next line. After stitching the strips, I pull the excess fabric loose from the foundation (freeing the extra stitches at the beginnings of the lines) and trim the excess fabric to a scant $1/4''$ seam allowance all at one time.

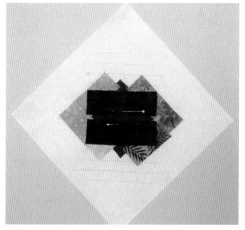

Adding diagonal strips and gauging the position of the new strip

8. Stitch the Pineapple strips, trim the threads and extra fabric, press, and pin in place as before.

End of round one

Tacking the corners down

9. Round 2 follows the same coloration as round 1: 2 short strips (1 light and 1 dark) opposite each other, 2 longer strips (1 light and 1 dark) also opposite each other, and finally the 2 Pineapple strips.

Note: The odd numbered segments on the pattern require the short strips and the even numbered segments require the long strips.

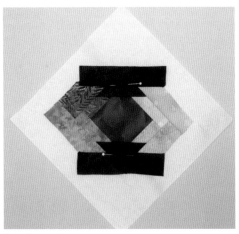
End of round two

10. Continue for 2 more rounds. Add a triangle to each Pineapple section to complete the block. Press the block firmly from the fabric side and then from the foundation side.

11. To anchor the floppy corners, place the block in the sewing machine with the foundation side up and stitch 4–5 *long* stitches in each of the 2 big corners (similar to a tailor tack) to hold the loose fabric against the foundation.

12. Trim the outside of the block to a $^1/_4$″ seam allowance on all sides.

13. Make 36 blocks and join them following the assembly diagram (page 47), rotating them to create the patterns of light and dark.

14. I bordered the quilt with $^1/_4$″-wide navy strips (both used in the Pineapple sections) and a $3^1/_2$″-wide string border made from the leftover light Log Cabin strips.

15. To make the string border, I drew parallel lines $^1/_2$″ apart on four $3^1/_2$″ × 36″ freezer-paper foundations and pieced them using *under* pressed piecing (see page 13). You could also choose to piece these with random-sized strips using *top* pressed piecing.

16. The corners were pure serendipity when I realized I could use horizontal and vertical strips overlapping in a Log Cabin format, repeating the design within the quilt. They were pieced on separate foundations using the pattern on page 47. Begin with the small square in the corner, and then add the logs using *under* pressed piecing. Sew these to each end of the top and bottom string borders.

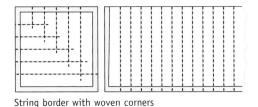
String border with woven corners

17. Assemble the layers, quilt, and bind as desired. I quilted both by hand and machine, emphasizing the design areas of the quilt.

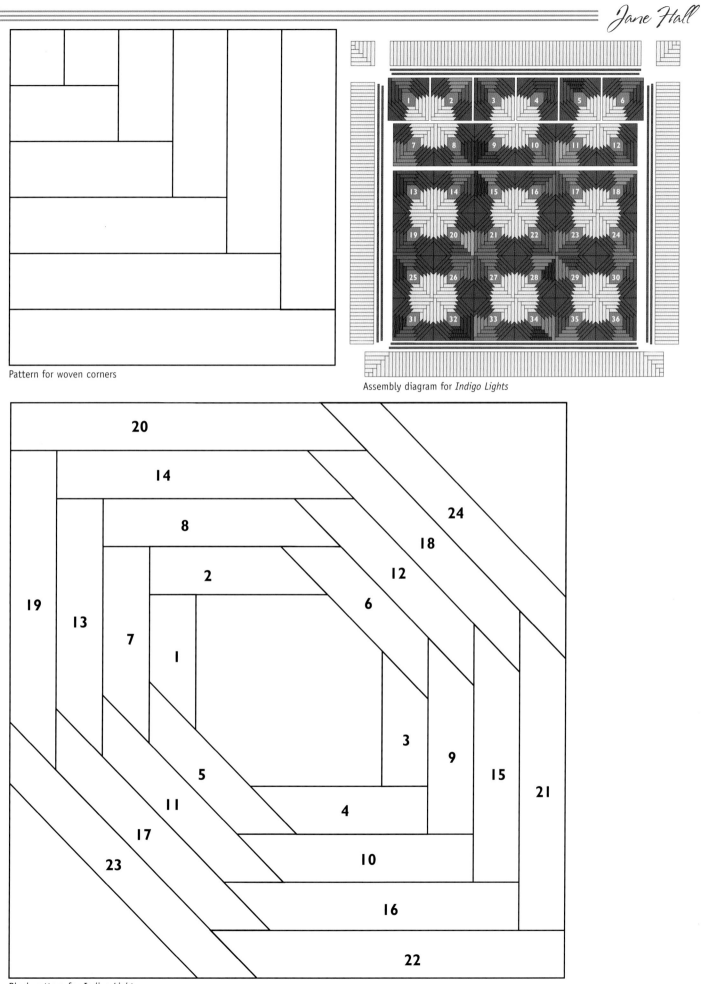

Pattern for woven corners

Assembly diagram for *Indigo Lights*

Block pattern for *Indigo Lights*

Barbara Barber

Pressed piecing, both *top* and *under*, was used from the beginning on whole blocks, starting in the center, at a corner, or on a side. Pressed piecing has a built-in geometric limitation—it is not possible to proceed when the next piece to be added has a cross-seam. There is no way to set in pieces on a foundation. This is most likely why patterns for foundations were limited to strings, crazy patches, and the Log Cabin family, all pieced on whole blocks.

Using all quilt patterns became possible once we realized that when pressed piecing could not continue, we could cut patterns apart, press piece on the parts, and then rejoin the segments. Foundation piecing, which so empowers us with its precision, could now be applied to long skinny points, multiple triangles, and all the complex patterns that are so appealing but may seem out of reach.

Many of the projects in this book are made by breaking up a design into segments for easy foundation piecing. Whether the design is simple or very complicated, it just takes a little time to get into the mind-set of figuring out the best places to divide a block.

Barbara Barber has become known in the quilt world for her designs with long skinny points, as well as for the whimsical quilt *Goato and Friends*. She has an intriguing technique for working with rings and has concocted a fantastic quilt that will let you try her method.

Barbara Barber, of Andover, England, is a full-time quilter, teacher, and lecturer and a master of design, color, and machine quilting. Her quilts have been widely exhibited worldwide and have won numerous awards, including several bests of show. She travels and teaches internationally and is constantly developing new techniques so quilters can create complex designs.

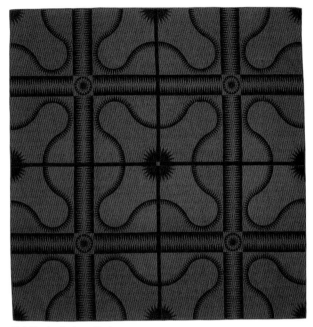

Solstice by Barbara Barber

RING PIECING

In 1991, because I could not find the right bedcover for our redecorated bedroom, I decided to make a quilt. I enjoyed sewing, but quilting had never interested me. Like so many others, after taking a few stitches for that first quilt, I was hooked for life and loving every minute of it.

I devoured every book I could find about quiltmaking. Because I was self-taught, this was the only way that I could learn about all the different aspects. I came across the paper-piecing technique and bypassed it. In the end, I got into paper piecing in the same way that I got into quiltmaking in general: it was simply a means to an end. By 1992 my enthusiasm was boundless, and it was during this time that I first drew up the design for my quilt *Solstice*.

It was an ambitious design and I certainly did not have the necessary knowledge or skills to make a quilt based on it, but I really did love the design and kept trying to devise methods of making it. This is when the notion of paper piecing kept coming back to me. Straight sections of triangles could be easily sewn on paper patterns to produce very sharp points. I could see how this same technique could be used to piece the curved sections for *Solstice*.

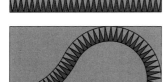

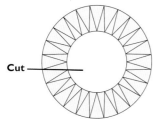

Straight and curved sections of points

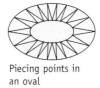

Piecing points in an oval

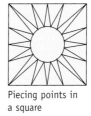

Piecing points in a square

Piecing points in a free-form shape

I saw that paper piecing would work for both the straight and the curved sections because they have a beginning and an end. But it would not work for the setting squares in the sashing, which were complete circles, because there was no beginning and no end to the continuous curved piecing for the circles. I soon figured out that I could simply cut through the circle of piecing to make a ring with a starting and finishing point. The center could then be appliquéd in place.

Cut

Setting block for sashing square with cut

The more I thought about it, the more possibilities I could see for this ring piecing. It would allow one to piece sharp points or wedges into virtually any shape that had a center with a ring of piecing around it: triangles, squares, hexagons, and ovals as well as free-form shapes. This is where paper and ring piecing combine to produce sharper points than would be possible using any other technique.

Piecing points in a triangle

Piecing points in a hexagon

This method of putting multiple rings together allowed me to make my quilt *Solstice*, and it became the subject of my first book and one of my favorite subjects to teach. Do not be discouraged if you find it confusing at first. It is a fun and rewarding technique, and I suggest you try the single-ring piecing technique in a small block, which is actually the center of a large quilt, as a learning exercise. The multiple-ring piecing in the quilt that follows will become much more straightforward.

Before starting to sew, starch your fabrics well, not just applying a small amount of starch. Make the mental comparison of working with either a tissue or a piece of index card to sew a block. Experiment with your own particular type of starch, but I urge you to try piecing with really stiff fabrics just once.

Bubble Gum Burst

By Barbara Barber
Block size: $12^1/_2{''} \times 12^1/_2{''}$

Materials

FABRIC

- Fabric A for star: $^3/_8$ yard
- Fabric B for star background: $^1/_2$ yard
- Background for block background: $^1/_2$ yard
- Contrasting fabric (or Fabric A): small scrap at least $5{''} \times 5{''}$ for appliquéd center circle
- Backing: $^1/_2$ yard
- Batting: $17{''} \times 17{''}$

OTHER SUPPLIES

- Paper for foundations
- Freezer paper
- Paper clips

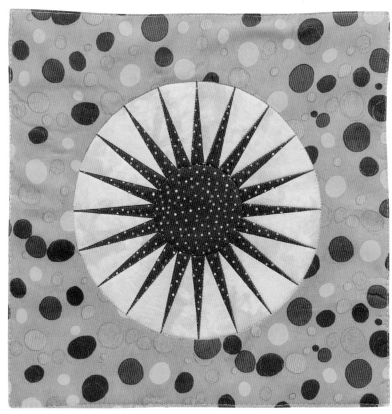

A whimsical introduction to single-ring piecing with long sharp points and perfect precision

Separate the freezer paper from the pattern sheet. Freezer paper will be used only for the outer background ring.

3. From the leftover pattern, cut out the template for the star center, cutting on the dotted line that lies $1/4''$ outside the solid line of the inner center circle.

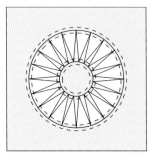

Cut out freezer-paper template for background; cut out paper template for center circle.

Preparing the foundations

Make 2 photocopies of the single-ring piecing block (pattern on the pullout). It is a multipattern combining 3 separate sections in 1 drawing. The solid lines on the drawing are the seamlines where the sections join, and the dotted lines on each side of the solid lines are the cutting lines for the different sections.

I prefer to work with photocopies of the pattern on ordinary paper rather than tracing each section onto freezer paper. I use freezer paper only for the background template.

PREPARING THE TEMPLATES FOR THE BACKGROUND SQUARE AND CENTER CIRCLE

1. Lightly iron a sheet of freezer paper over the printed side of 1 of the patterns. Trace the center circle and the outer circle. Mark each point of the star and the quarter-circle points as well.

2. Cut exactly on the dotted line that lies $1/4''$ inside the outer solid circle line to make the template for the background. The points of the star will be cut off and the lines that you drew will be left like minutes on a clock face around the edge of the freezer-paper circle.

PREPARING THE FOUNDATION FOR THE INNER RING

1. On the second pattern copy, mark the A and B sections and cut out the star circle pattern $1/8''$ *outside* the outer dotted line. The dotted line will be the final cutting line for trimming after the piecing is complete, and adding a bit more to the seam allowance is just insurance. Cut out the inner circle just outside the innermost dotted line. You now have a ring ready to sew on.

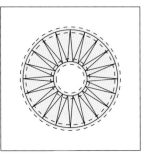

Cut out foundation for ring with points.

2. Cut through the ring, into the center, exactly on 1 of the straight lines for the points.

Cutting through the ring

3. Roll the paper ring in on itself to make it easier to handle and to decrease the chances of tearing the paper during sewing. Use a large paper clip to keep it rolled up while you work, leaving about 5″ free at the end.

Cutting the fabric

- Fabric A: Cut 1 strip 5″ × the width of the fabric, then cut into 20 strips 5″ × 1½″.
- Fabric B: Cut 2 strips 5″ × the width of the fabric, then cut into 20 strips 5″ × 2½″.
- Fabric for background: Cut 1 square 13″ × 13″.
- Fabric for the center: Cut 1 square 5″ × 5″.

Piecing the ring

1. Place 1 A piece and 1 B piece right sides together with the long edges even on 1 side. It does not matter which end of the roll you start sewing on—just make sure you put the narrow fabric on piece A or the wider fabric on piece B. Place the rolled paper ring on top of these fabrics with a ¼″ seam allowance beyond the solid stitching line. Check that the ends of the fabric pieces protrude beyond the top and bottom edges of the paper ring.

2. Stitch, with a small stitch size, from the top edge of the fabrics down along the solid seamline and through to the other edge of the fabrics.

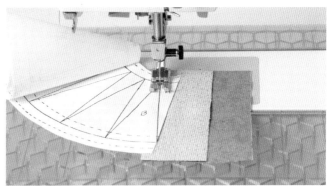

Positioning the paper roll and sewing on the line

3. Remove from the machine and finger-press the fabrics open. Trim the fabric very close to the inner and outer curved edges of the paper ring. On the straight end where you cut through the ring, trim the fabric to ¼″ beyond the edge of the paper to form the seam allowance when the ring is rejoined. I like to baste along the straight edge with a very large stitch, as this makes sewing the ring back together much easier.

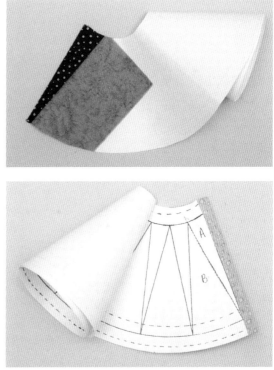

Fabrics A and B trimmed and pressed open

The first 2 pieces of a ring are always added in this way. The rest of the pieces in the ring are added in an alternating sequence.

4. Position the foundation over the next piece of fabric A, with a scant ¼″ seam allowance extending beyond the line toward the paper roll that has not yet been pieced.

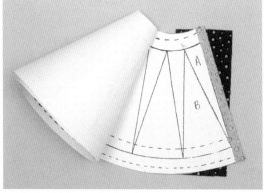

Positioning fabric A under foundation

5. Stitch on the line. Before opening the piece, trim the seam allowance for the seam you have just sewn to ¼″. Open the piece, press, and trim the curved edges as you did before.

6. Continue to add pieces in this manner, alternating fabric A and B until you have completed the ring. Trim the straight edge of the final piece, adding a ¼″ seam allowance beyond the edge of the paper. Baste along the paper.

7. To accurately join the ring back into a full circle, insert straight pins just off the paper in the seam allowance, at the beginning and ending point of the ring. Use a pricking movement until you are able to find and push the pins through in the right place. Then pin with the pins perpendicular to the seamline and sew along the edge of the paper pattern.

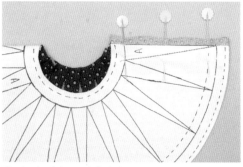

Pinning back into a full circle

8. Press the seam allowance in the same direction as the rest of the seams.

9. Using scissors, cut exactly on the curved, dotted cutting line around the outer and inner edges of the ring, removing any excess fabric and foundation.

10. Using the template for the center circle, cut out the circle. Use whichever technique you wish to appliqué the center onto the ring. I use a heavily starched fabric and the paper template for the center to make a perfect circle, which can be attached to the ring by hand or machine.

Preparing the background square

1. Fold the square of fabric into fourths and press the freezer-paper template on it, matching the quarter marks. Cut out the center circle from the fabric.

2. Match the marks on the freezer paper to the points of the pieced star and pin in place, right sides together.

3. Stitch along the solid curved seamline with the paper pattern on top and using a small stitch size.

4. Press the seam away from the pieced ring.

Multiple-ring piecing

After you work out the techniques for making a single-ring design, it is easy to move to multiple-ring piecing. Now that you have mastered the single ring, try this 30″ 4-ring block.

4-ring block, 30″ × 30″

Materials (for 1 large block)

FABRIC

- Yellow: $2^{1}/_{8}$ yards
- Red: 1 yard
- Blue: $^{3}/_{4}$ yard

OTHER SUPPLIES

- Paper and freezer paper for foundations
- Starch
- Paper clips

Preparing the foundation

1. The pattern is printed in 2 sections: the center (single-ring piecing block on the pullout) and the pattern for the 3 outer rings (on the pullout). Assemble a whole pattern from these parts by copying or tracing the center plus 8 copies of the 3 ring wedges. Overlap small copies and trace or have large photocopies made. You will need 2 complete pattern sheets for the block. I feel that photocopying is more accurate than tracing for this technique.

2. Cut apart 1 pattern on the appropriate dotted lines, to produce the center, ring 3, and ring 5. Cut slightly outside the inner- and outer-edge dotted line for #3 and #5 as you did with the single ring.

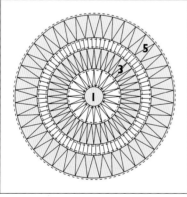

Cutting diagram for first set of rings

3. Join 2 pieces of freezer paper together and cut out a $30^{1}/_{2}{''} \times 30^{1}/_{2}{''}$ square. Center the second pattern onto the freezer paper square and press. Cut out the background (6) slightly outside the inner dashed line (see page 50 and the pullout). Pull off the freezer paper from the middle and cut out rings 2 and 4.

Again, cut slightly outside the inner- and outer-edge dotted line for rings 2 and 4.

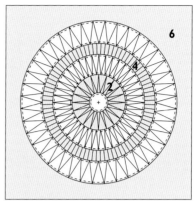

Cutting diagrams for the second set of rings

Cutting the fabric

Prepare all the fabrics by starching them well. The dimensions for cut pieces are generous. See pattern on the pullout for location of pieces in the block.

YELLOW

- Cut 1 square $30^{1}/_{2}{''} \times 30^{1}/_{2}{''}$.
- Cut 1 strip $5{''} \times$ the width of the fabric, then cut into 20 pieces $5{''} \times 2{''}$ for B.
- Cut 2 strips $4^{1}/_{2}{''} \times$ the width of the fabric, then cut into 40 pieces $4^{1}/_{2}{''} \times 1^{1}/_{2}{''}$ for C.
- Cut 3 strips $5^{1}/_{2}{''} \times$ the width of the fabric, then cut into 40 pieces $5^{1}/_{2}{''} \times 2^{3}/_{4}{''}$ for H.

RED

- Cut 2 strips $4^{1}/_{2}{''} \times$ the width of the fabric, then cut into 40 pieces $4^{1}/_{2}{''} \times 2{''}$ for D.
- Cut 2 strips $3{''} \times$ the width of the fabric, then cut into 40 pieces $3{''} \times 2{''}$ for F.
- Cut 2 strips $5^{1}/_{2}{''} \times$ the width of the fabric, then cut into 40 pieces $5^{1}/_{2}{''} \times 2{''}$ for G.

BLUE

- Cut 2 strips $5{''} \times$ the width of the fabric, then cut into 40 pieces $5{''} \times 1^{1}/_{2}{''}$ for A.
- Cut 2 strips $3{''} \times$ the width of the fabric, then cut into 40 pieces $3{''} \times 1{''}$ for E.
- Cut 1 square $5{''} \times 5{''}$ for center.

Construction

1. Prepare and construct the 4 rings, the freezer-paper background template, and the center appliqué template just as you did for the single ring.

a. Roll each of the rings up and secure with a paper clip to make piecing easier.

b. Piece all 4 of the rings for the block and trim them exactly on the outer dotted cutting line, removing any excess fabric and foundation before rejoining them to form a circle again.

c. Iron the freezer paper onto the background square, mark all the registration marks onto the fabric, and cut the center circle out along the edge of the freezer paper.

d. Using the paper template for the center, prepare and appliqué the center onto the smallest ring. Do not remove the paper from the pieced ring yet.

2. Assemble the block beginning from the outside.

a. Sew the outer ring into the background, matching the registration lines. Lay it flat on a work surface and carefully remove the paper from the outer ring.

b. Match, pin, and sew each of the remaining 3 rings into position, one by one, as you did for the first. The little cut-off tips of the points from each ring will help with the positioning.

c. Remove the paper from each ring once it is completely sewn into the background and before starting to sew the following ring into position.

One block would make a marvelous wall hanging or a center for a medallion quilt. Or consider going even larger. I designed *Old Yeller*, a quilt in strong, vibrant colors using 4 of these blocks, with an outer border of small single-ring blocks.

Old Yeller (detail) designed by Barbara Barber, made by Keith Nuehring, see full quilt on page 117.

Eileen Sullivan

Eileen Sullivan uses *under* pressed piecing in yet another way to create her nontraditional, innovative designs. Since the early 1990s, she has consistently designed elegant and appealing flowers and plants. Her cleverness in dividing the pattern into easily pieced segments, making them accessible to quilters of all skill levels, has led her to designing patterns, along with teaching and lecturing.

Eileen Sullivan, of Alpharetta, Georgia, trained as an art educator and taught art in public schools for many years. She is known for her strong, innovative pieced designs, and her quilts have been exhibited worldwide and have won many prestigious awards. *Peace Lily* was the launching point for her pattern design company. She teaches and travels nationally.

When Grandmother's Lily Garden Blooms (detail) by Eileen Sullivan. Photo courtesy of American Quilter's Society, see full quilt on page 118. Photo by Charles R. Lynch.

INNOVATIVE DESIGN

My style of working is a combination of preplanning and a relaxed method of fabric usage. I don't spend time measuring, cutting, or trimming as I go along. I like to refer to my method as self-cleaning. After each new fabric is added, the freezer paper is folded back to the sewn line, excess fabric is whacked away, and the new piece, even if irregular, is ironed to the freezer paper to control it. It doesn't matter how teeny a piece is: you never actually have to cut and handle that. It's just *one more seam*!

I'm often asked how I came to work the way I do. My response is, "I didn't invent it; I just pushed it to work for me." Working with a foundation is not new. How we do it, however, can be. Many of us in this field have a slightly different view of what a foundation can do for us. For me, it's the master plan as well as the fabric stabilizer, and it allows me to use fabrics and shapes freely. I refer to my technique as a sew-and-flip method, because that's actually what you do—line the fabric up, sew it on the line, then flip it into place. While not a sophisticated term, it is descriptive of the process.

When designing, I treat the entire project, including borders, as a whole, then subdivide as necessary for construction. Borders should not be an afterthought but an integral part of the entire composition. Design elements that extend into the border can create a very dynamic statement. I do not leave a paper seam allowance around each section because it's easier to draw this way. Almost as importantly, when joining two sections together I'm only sewing through the fabrics, not an additional two layers of paper that would also have to be removed later.

The most exciting and often frustrating part of a new design is getting started. When I approach a new flower design, for example, I have to fully understand what is unique to that particular image. Rough sketches determine general compositional elements, and then the dissection process begins. I work from the whole to its smaller parts, breaking units and sections apart as needed to comply with the necessary sewing sequence. Simplification is the greatest challenge. I have to be able to define what I need with the fewest possible pieces. I have been fascinated with puzzles for years, and this method of working appeals to me.

Fabric selection is critical to success. To create realism, textures and values must flow smoothly to provide shading. I always work with an eye to value and contrast. There *are* reasons to buy fabric all the time—we do not have the luxury other artists have of mixing paint to achieve the perfect color. My studio is a perfect testament to that! I tell students to pull out *everything* in a particular color family, arrange it by value, and pull out value duplicates. Eventually, the range of four or five fabrics to use becomes obvious.

I often ask students if they understand how to construct a Log Cabin block on a foundation. Even if they've never done it, they get the concept. However, the minute I begin to move the lines so they are no longer parallel to each other, the concept gets lost. It's the moving and manipulating that gives one the ability to create almost any image. And that's the part I enjoy most.

Summer Pleasures

By Eileen Sullivan

Quilt size: $15^1/_2{''} \times 19^1/_2{''}$
Block size: 8 different-sized rectangles

Materials

FABRICS

- Scraps, up to $^1/_8$ yard each, of 4 shades of 4–5 colors for flowers
- Small amounts of accents for flower centers
- Assorted greens (3–4 each darks, mediums, and lights) totaling $^1/_4$ yard each value
- $^1/_4$ yard sky fabric
- $^1/_2$ yard fabric for border, cut as follows: 4 strips cut 4″ wide from lengthwise grain (use the remaining fabric for Blocks 7 and 8)
- Backing: 20″ × 23″
- Batting: 20″ × 23″
- Binding: $^1/_4$ yard

OTHER SUPPLIES

- Freezer paper for foundations
- Mechanical pencil and thin clear ruler
- Colored pencils
- Highlighter
- Small craft knife

About the foundation pattern

Each block in the project follows the same format. The block is broken down into units (A, B, C, etc.). Each unit may be broken down further into several sections. These are referred to as A1, A2, and so on. Heavy broken lines indicate where the units break apart. Smaller broken lines indicate the sections. All these broken lines are cut-apart lines. The solid lines are stitching lines within the sections.

Do not be intimidated by small pieces. The foundation is just that, a foundation on which pieces are added in order, not cut apart into individual pieces. It's simply sewing another line. If you wish to work larger, photocopy all the blocks with the same percentage of enlargement (on the same machine and at the same time). Once you are comfortable doing one section,

Summer Pleasures. This quilt is an outgrowth of my workshop "How Does Your Garden Grow?" combining various flower blocks to create projects for small quilts or garments.

the process is the same for all the others. The instructions that follow use Block 3 as an example.

Because you are drawing on the dull side of the freezer paper and attaching the fabric to the other side, the pattern and the assembly diagram are reversed from the finished quilt. This is a true mirror image.

Preparing the foundations

Freezer paper for foundations is readily available, inexpensive, and controls bias edges as you work, eliminating distortion. The time spent tracing is adequately rewarded when sewing begins.

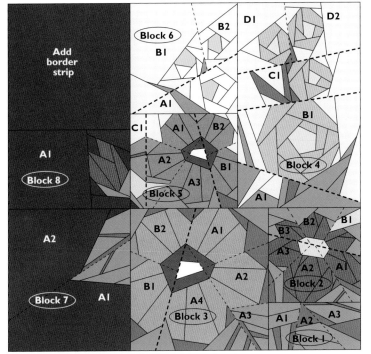

Assembly diagram as paper foundations will be placed

1. Tape freezer paper shiny side down, dull side up, over each block pattern (on the pullout). Use a mechanical pencil and thin clear ruler to trace. *Do not use a rotary ruler to trace the lines since they cast shadows and can distort the tracing.* Include all unit and section numbers as well as sewing order and fabric to be used.

2. When the tracing is complete, *trim away all excess freezer paper from the outer edges.* Fabrics will always extend beyond the paper to create a seam allowance. Joining sections is easier when there isn't a layer of paper in the seam allowance.

3. Before cutting any units apart, be sure to do the following:

- Use a highlighting marker around the outer edges of the block. This will be a visual heads-up to leave plenty of extra fabric at the outer edges for squaring up after the block is completed.

- Use colored pencils to add reference marks (hash marks perpendicular to the line) in a few places on each broken line. These are critical in the rejoining process. Use a different color on each line to avoid confusion.

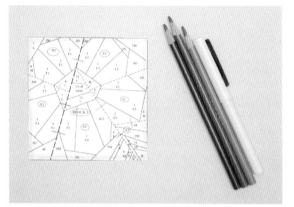

Highlighting and reference marks on foundation

4. Using a breakaway or craft knife, cut apart the units within each block along the heavy dashed lines. Begin with unit A and cut into further individual sections along the lighter dashed lines, if needed. Be careful not to misplace the small sections. I like to pin them to the corner of my ironing board for security.

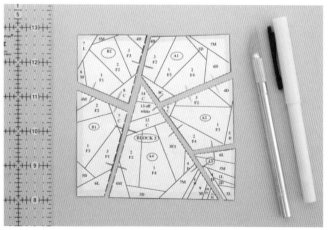

Foundation cut into sections

Fabric selection

1. Each flower is made up of 4 shades, from darkest to lightest in a smooth progression. The darkest shade is referred to as *F1*, the next, *F2*, then *F3*, and the lightest is *F4*. Make an index card with each fabric swatch coded this way and keep it at your machine for easy reference.

2. The centers of the flowers are referred to as *C*. Use more than 1 shade if desired.

3. All greens are grouped into 3 piles—light, medium, and dark—and are referred to as *L*, *M*, and *D*. Use as many fabrics as you wish, and use them randomly. Try to include interesting textures for variety and interest.

4. The background is sky and is called *S*.

5. Border fabric is indicated by *Border*.

Fabric selections

Construction

SECTIONS

Set your machine for a shorter than normal stitch length (16–18 stitches per inch, or 1.75 metric). This helps to perforate the paper for easier removal and provides stronger seams. Use a sharp rather than universal needle.

Tip

Do *not* try to cut individual shapes. You will be wrong more often than right! Instead, use "workable size" pieces of each fabric, such as fat strips or pieces 5″ × 7″.

1. The fabric for piece 1 is simply ironed in place, with the wrong side of the fabric adhering to the freezer paper. Take the freezer paper *to the fabric*, position, iron in place, and *then* "rough cut away" what is not needed.

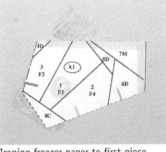

Ironing freezer paper to first piece of fabric

2. Place the fabric for piece 2 right sides together with piece 1, having a straight edge parallel to the sewing line, approximately $1/4''$ beyond the sewing line. It is easier if you hold your piece so that the sewing line is horizontal in front of you and the second fabric is hanging down and the area to be covered is above.

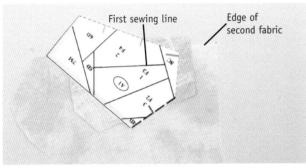

Second piece added

Tip

If you are concerned about the fit of the piece, take a moment to pin check by pinning on the line and flipping the new fabric to see where it lies. It's easier to unpin and realign than rip out.

You can always fold the freezer paper back to the sewing line between pieces 1 and 2 and pretrim the allowance to $1/4''$. Then line up the straight edge of your fabric with this. Once you're comfortable with aligning the new fabric you can simply skip this step to speed things up.

3. Stitch on the line, starting and ending 1 or 2 stitches past where another line crosses. When sewing off the paper, continue stitching through what will be the seam allowance.

4. After sewing, fold the foundation back to the sewn line and eyeball a $1/4''$ seam allowance parallel to the sewing line and trim.

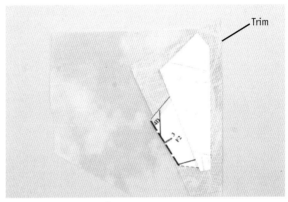

Trimming excess seam allowance

5. Open up the second piece and, after ironing it in place, rough cut away generously beyond the sewing lines, making sure it covers all that it needs to. No need to be fussy, as this is a self-cleaning project.

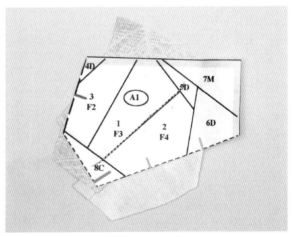

Second piece ironed in place and trimmed

6. Continue adding pieces in this manner until the section is complete.

Tip

When the line for a pointy shape goes *off the paper*, sew much further than you think you should to allow for the seam allowance. It is almost impossible to "eyeball" this.

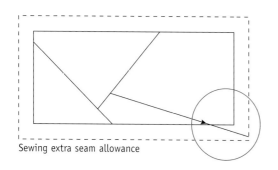

Sewing extra seam allowance

UNITS

1. When the sections within a unit are complete, use a rotary cutter and ruler to trim *only* the sides that will join others (those with the reference marks on them), exactly ¼″ beyond the paper. Leave all outer edges (the highlighted ones) alone for now.

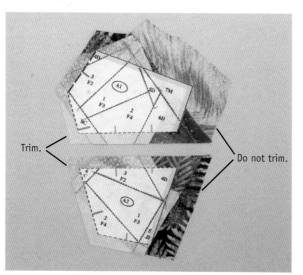

Trim.   Do not trim.

Trimmed sections, ready to join

2. Align the sections to be joined, keeping the trimmed sides even, and place a pin through a reference mark. It should come out *exactly* at the same point on the back side. Adjust until you get it just right.

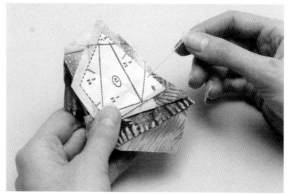

Pin through a reference mark.

3. Pin parallel to the paper, with the heads of the pins toward you and the points toward the machine. Add 1 more anchor pin at the end out of the way of the sewing.

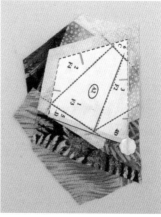

Pinning sections together

4. Sew *right next to the edge of the paper*, removing pins as you come to them.

5. Press the seam allowance to the side of least resistance, or open to help reduce bulk.

6. Join sections to complete units. Join the units to complete the block.

SQUARING UP

When a block is complete, use a square-up ruler to trim the first 2 adjoining sides exactly ¼″ beyond the paper. This will give you a perfect 90° angle. Then, referring to the size the block is *supposed* to finish to plus the ¼″ seam allowance on all sides, rotate the block and use your ruler to trim the last 2 sides.

If you sewed with a slight variance on an inner seam, correcting the outer edge correspondingly will make the finished project go together more easily, since there are few if any serious matching joins. The finished size does matter.

Final assembly

(Refer to assembly diagram, page 57.)

1. Complete Blocks 1 and 2 and join them together.

2. Complete Block 3 and join it to 1 and 2. Set aside.

3. Complete Block 4.

4. Complete Blocks 5 and 6. Join these together. Add Block 4.

5. Join 1/2/3 to 4/5/6.

6. Complete Blocks 7 and 8 (border blocks). Join them together and add the $4^{1}/_{2}'' \times 4^{1}/_{2}''$ border square to the top of Block 8. Join this border to the project.

7. Add the other side border ($4^{1}/_{2}'' \times 11^{1}/_{2}''$), then the top and bottom borders ($4^{1}/_{2}'' \times 16''$).

8. All freezer paper remains in place until straight-grain borders are added. Remove the freezer paper carefully, using tweezers as needed. When all paper is removed, carefully steam press. Layer with batting and backing and baste. Quilt minimally, outlining flower edges, centers, and leaves. Square up the quilt and add the binding.

Folded Foundations

An innovative way to think about foundations is to recognize that they do not always have to be *sewn on* to be used effectively. For differing reasons, and using differing techniques, three quiltmakers have come up with efficient ways to piece with foundations by folding them.

One technique involves stitching segments on a creased *whole* foundation. This unique method eliminates the difficulty of matching points and lines when joining separate block segments together.

In the other two, the foundations are not stitched through but are folded back at the seamline just before stitching. The fabric is pressed back onto the freezer paper after the seam is stitched, which provides foundation stability.

This approach addresses a major complaint about pressed piecing in general and freezer-paper foundations in particular—the tedious task of removing the foundation. Although freezer paper is popular—because it holds fabric firmly and helps ensure accuracy even with difficult patterns—removing it is not only tiresome but can distort the stitching. Judy Mathieson, widely known for her Mariner's Compass designs, has a brilliant solution to this problem.

Judy Mathieson

Judy Mathieson, of Sebastopol, California, has been teaching quiltmaking since 1977, both nationally and internationally. Her quilts have won many awards, and her *Nautical Stars* was included in *The Twentieth Century's Best American Quilts*. Her favorite patterns are Mariner's Compass–style stars, and she has written several books about them.

PERFORATED FREEZER-PAPER FOUNDATIONS

I have always loved precision-pieced quilts, and foundation techniques can help quilters be successful with my favorite patterns, Mariner's Compass-style stars. These stars have lots of bias edges and sharp points, and they will not lie flat if the sewing doesn't respect the lines of the pattern.

I must confess that I resisted foundation piecing for a long time. The techniques I learned seemed backward and hard to teach to others. I didn't like to tear out the paper at the end or lose control over the final direction of the seam allowances. I often made mistakes in estimating the size of the fabric pieces used to cover the paper, and then all the tiny stitches were almost impossible to take out. I frequently just tossed the whole segment if I made a mistake!

In 1995 I wrote *Mariner's Compass Quilts: New Directions*. I used a foundation method that involved making freezer-paper patterns for each of the patches in the design. I sewed along the edge of the freezer paper *through the fabrics only*. No tearing and no little stitches, but lots of paper pieces. However, as I worked with that technique, I discovered another method that seemed to eliminate all the things I didn't like about foundation piecing. It was also more efficient.

I call this technique Perforated Freezer-Paper Foundations. An unthreaded sewing machine is used to punch holes in the seamlines of several pieces of paper at the same time. The first fabric patch in the piecing sequence is ironed to the freezer paper, which is then folded back on the perforated line. After the second fabric patch is aligned, the stitching goes only through the fabrics, using a regular stitch length. Since the paper pattern is folded back, the fabric patches can be easily checked to see if they are fully covering the paper. The paper can be pulled away temporarily to realign

Marbled Stars (detail) by Judy Mathieson, see full quilt on page 119.

seam allowances. When the segment is complete, the foundations can be gently pulled away and used several more times.

While I created this technique to help add precision when piecing the complex stars, it can be used for almost any foundation-piecing design. I hope it finds a place in your bag of tricks.

Little Fishes Too

By Judy Mathieson

Quilt size: 19″ × 19″
Block size: 10″ × 10″ (8″ circle)

Materials

FABRIC

- Star points: 4 strips $2^{1}/_{2}″ \times 3^{3}/_{4}″$ of each of 2 different fabrics
- Background circle: $^{1}/_{8}$ yard of fabric to complement star points
- Background square: $^{1}/_{3}$ yard
- Star center and outer border corners: 1 square 3″ × 3″ for center and 4 squares $3^{1}/_{2}″ \times 3^{1}/_{2}″$ for corners of fabric to contrast with star points
- Inner border: $^{1}/_{4}$ yard for 4 strips $2″ \times 10^{1}/_{2}″$ of wavy stripe fabric to coordinate with star block
- Inner border corners: $^{1}/_{8}$ yard for 4 squares 2″ × 2″ of fabric to coordinate with inner border

This small Mariner's Compass Star quilt with novelty fish fabric in the border is easily and accurately constructed using folded freezer-paper foundations.

- Outer border: ¹/₄ yard for 4 strips 3¹/₂″ × 13¹/₂″ of novelty fish fabric (remaining yardage will be used for fish that are appliquéd to the finished quilt top)
- Backing: ³/₄ yard
- Batting: 23″ × 23″
- Binding: ⁵/₈ yard

OTHER SUPPLIES
- Freezer paper for foundations

Preparing the foundations

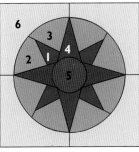

Mariner's Compass pattern

1. Trace or photocopy the 1, 2, 3, and 4 segments of the design on page 69 as 1 unit. Place the copy on a stack of 4 pieces of freezer paper, all with shiny sides up. Fasten the copy and the freezer paper together temporarily with staples or use the tip of a dry, hot iron at the Xs on the pattern to adhere the layers.

2. Set the stitch length on the sewing machine to 12–15 stitches per inch. Use an unthreaded sewing machine needle to stitch on each of the sewing lines of the pattern.

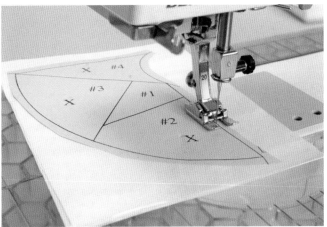

Stitch sewing lines of the pattern.

3. Remove the pattern for use at another time. Cut the freezer-paper foundations into the desired units on the perforated lines. If you are careful, you may be able to cut a whole stack at once. Label the dull side with piece numbers.

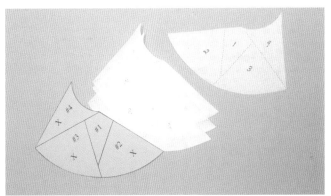

Trim foundation units

4. Use the original pattern to make a template on freezer paper for each shape within the unit. Add ¹/₂″ to each edge of each segment. Mark each template with the grain line and the number of pieces to cut (see diagrams on page 69). Use the templates to cut the fabrics. It isn't necessary to cut these fabrics precisely, as the ¹/₂″ allows for the positioning necessary with foundation techniques. Seam allowances will be trimmed later.

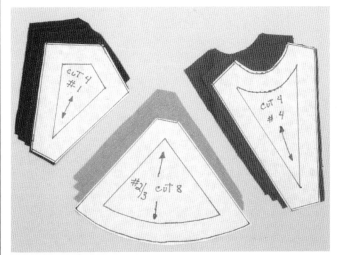

Templates with ¹/₂″ seam allowance added

Piecing

1. Iron each pattern unit, shiny side down, to a piece of muslin or scrap fabric, then remove it before you begin piecing. This removes the shine from the freezer paper and helps the presser foot glide more easily as you sew. Use a hot, dry iron to adhere the once-shiny side of the freezer paper to the wrong side of fabric 1.

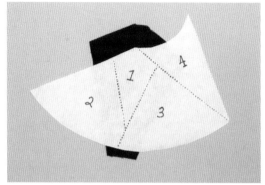

Attaching foundation unit to fabric 1

2. Fold the freezer paper back on the perforated line between paper areas 1 and 2 to expose the seamline. Place fabric 2 right sides together with fabric 1. Check to make sure the paper area 2 is completely covered by fabric 2.

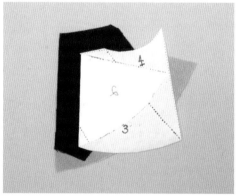

Fabric 2 placed right sides together with fabric 1; foundation folded back at the seamline

3. Stitch along the edge of the folded freezer paper, through the 2 fabrics, using a regular stitch length. If the presser foot hangs up on the sticky side of the freezer paper, place a strip of paper along the edge of the freezer paper to block the sticky side.

Stitching through the two fabrics; strip of paper is a sewing aid

4. Trim the seam allowance to $1/4''$, fold the paper back, and press the fabric to the freezer paper. If fabric 1 is darker than fabric 2, grade the seam so that the lighter fabric extends beyond the darker fabric.

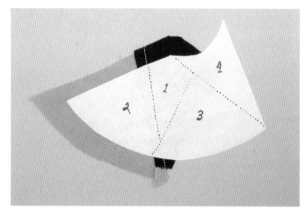

Fabric pressed onto paper area 2

5. Add pieces 3 and 4 in the same way: fold the paper on the perforations along the line to be stitched and position the fabric right sides together with the previous addition, making sure that it covers the appropriate area. Stitch along the edge of the folded freezer paper through the fabric layers. Trim and press.

6. Trim and press the seam allowance away from fabric 4, toward the background fabric (fabrics 1 and 3). I like to press all the seam allowances toward the background fabric so my star points are crisp and free of seam allowances. I adjust the direction of the seams as I go along by temporarily pulling the freezer paper back about $1/2''$ from the seam.

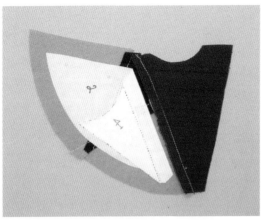

Adjusting direction of seam allowance into star point

7. Press paper area 4 back over fabric 4. Press and trim, leaving a $\frac{1}{4}$″ seam allowance on all sides.

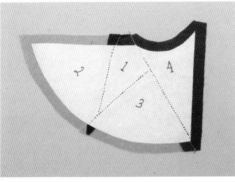

Completed unit, trimmed and pressed

8. When you have completed 4 of these segments, pin them together at the intersections in sets of 2 along the side of fabric 4 to ensure that your stitching creates a sharp point at the tip of the star.

To avoid sewing through the paper on the back of the segments, temporarily pull the freezer paper away (about $\frac{1}{2}$″) on the back side of the 2-segment unit. Stitch on the front side, then press the seam allowances toward the background fabric.

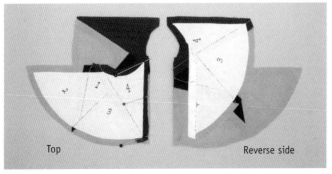

Top   Reverse side

Units pinned together

9. Join the 2-unit segments together, making a circle, and press well.

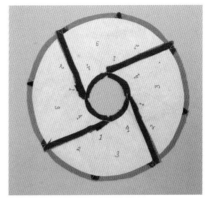

Four units joined

10. Remove the paper foundations by pulling them gently away from the fabrics. Check seams for fraying as you remove the papers. Pull the paper in a different direction if you encounter fraying. You can usually reuse foundations several times after removing any loose threads.

11. Trace the center circle 5 on page 69 onto freezer paper and cut a fabric circle with a $\frac{1}{4}$″ seam allowance. Pin the pattern shiny side up to the wrong side of the fabric.

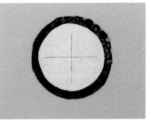

Use the tip of a hot iron to press (baste) the seam allowance to the freezer-paper circle. Fold the circle into quarters to position and appliqué it into place.

Assembly

1. The completed star can be appliquéd to a 10½″ background square, or you may use pattern piece 6 on page 69 to cut 4 background quarters. Sew the 4 pieces together and piece the star circle into the background.

Complete star circle ready for background

2. Stitch the inner borders to the vertical sides, and then the border strips with end corners to the top and bottom. Repeat with the outer border. Cut fish images from novelty fabric and appliqué in desired positions.

3. Layer the top with batting and backing. Quilt as desired or follow the suggested quilting diagram for the star block. I quilted in an extra set of points behind the pieced points. Finish with binding. I used bias binding but straight binding would also work.

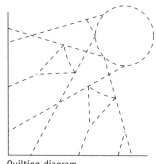

Quilting diagram

X **#4**

#5

#3

X

#1

#2

X

#6

Star block pattern

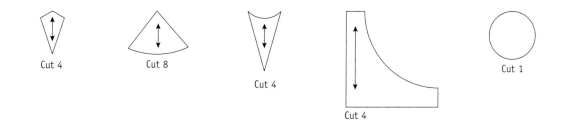

Cut 4   Cut 8   Cut 4   Cut 4   Cut 1

Barb Vlack

A second quilter who works with freezer-paper foundations and loves the idea of not stitching through them has changed Judy Mathieson's folded method slightly to adapt it to her computer designs.

Barb Vlack, of St. Charles, Illinois, has become internationally known for her work with The Electric Quilt Company. She travels, teaches, and has written several books dealing with designing quilts on the computer. She labels her style innovative traditional because she loves to make traditional patterns look different.

COMPUTER-PRINTED FREEZER-PAPER FOUNDATIONS

When I learned Judy Mathieson's foundation-piecing method with freezer paper, I was seriously impressed by its efficiency. With this new method of stitching the seams *next to the fold* of the freezer paper instead of on the line *through* the paper, all I could think of was why-didn't-we-think-of-this-before? The foundation is ironed to the block during construction and there is no stitching through the paper, so the dreaded task of tearing away the foundation after stitching is avoided. Another enormous advantage of folding freezer-paper foundations is that seam allowances can be pressed in the direction that will emphasize the designs as well as in the direction that will make seam intersections less bulky.

As I worked with this technique, I couldn't help but adapt it to fit my style of designing the quilt and blocks on the computer, then printing the pattern from a quilt-designing software program (Electric Quilt). I knew I could print onto freezer paper with my inkjet printer, since I do that all the time with appliqué templates. The next logical step was to print out *foundations* onto freezer paper.

Many piecing patterns can be adapted to this method. I sometimes feel like an evangelist when I tout the reasons I love *folded* freezer-paper foundation piecing. The technique has offered me a quilting-life-changing experience!

I have used freezer-paper foundations to piece the triangles on the curve of a New York Beauty block, intricate units in Cynthia England's and Ruth McDowell's designs, and Mariner's Compass blocks with sharp points. Freezer-paper foundation piecing is wonderful for miniatures and stabilizes the multiple seams in pieced borders. Imagine peeling off the entire foundation in one sheet after the block is stitched instead of needing to use a magnifying glass and tweezers to rip out extra tiny pieces of foundation paper.

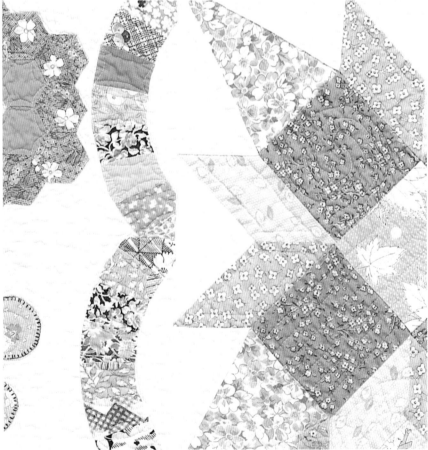

It's Chic to Be Shabby (detail) by Barb Vlack, see full quilt on page 122.

Experience with freezer-paper foundation piecing has shown that I can piece with scraps just large enough to cover the patch area and not pay attention to grain line. Other times, it is best to cut a shape from a template with attention to the grain line and at least a $^3/8''$ seam allowance just for a little insurance. I recommend this especially for odd-shaped pieces or triangles.

Every Which Way

By Barb Vlack

Quilt size: 34″ × 34″
Block sizes: 6″ × 6″ (center of quilt),
3″ × 3″ (blocks set on point for borders),
$4^1/4''$ × $4^1/4''$ (border corners)

Every Which Way. This simple-to-construct quilt uses an asymmetrical block that can be rotated to create several different layouts.

6″ block   3″ and $4^1/4''$ blocks

The blocks are colored differently on opposite sides of the diagonal line to create the pattern.

 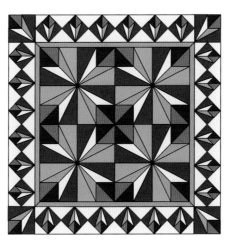 

Every Which Way—other possible versions

Materials

FABRIC

Choose values that clearly separate the design units of the blocks. Color values for each fabric below are listed in parenthesis.

- Purple: 1 yard (includes binding) (darkest)
- Medium blue: $^3/_8$ yard for center blocks (medium)
- Light gold: 1 yard (lightest)
- Dark gold: $^7/_8$ yard (medium)
- Light red: $^3/_8$ yard (secondary light)
- Dark red: $^3/_8$ yard (secondary dark)
- Backing: $1^1/_8$ yards
- Batting: 38″ × 38″

OTHER SUPPLIES

- Freezer paper for foundations
- Card-stock straightedge for folding (can be a bookmark or a postcard)
- Add-a-Quarter ruler (6″)
- Foil-wrapped pressing board (see Tip on page 73.)
- Optional: Edge-stitching presser foot, if your sewing machine has one
- Optional: Plastic pan scraper—it's handy for scraping lint off the freezer paper and helps to extend the life of the pattern (The edge of a credit card could also be used.)

Preparing the foundations

1. Use a computer program to scan or draw the patterns as shown on the pullout, and print them out. Check the accuracy in the size of the printout. My computer software allows me to print blocks in grayscale, which helps me keep track of where to place light and dark fabrics as I piece. (If you do not have drawing or scanning software, photocopy the patterns.)

2. Use a computer and *inkjet printer* to print the pattern onto the *dull* side of the freezer paper. Do *not* send freezer paper through a copy machine or a laser printer because heat could melt the waxy side. Print out 4 copies each of units A and B of the 6″ block (on the pullout), adding a $^1/_4$″ seam allowance around the segments/units. Because you can reuse the patterns, 4 copies should be plenty to make the 16 center blocks.

Tip

Flatten the freezer paper as much as possible and tape the leading edge of the freezer paper $^1/_4$″ down from the top of a regular piece of copy paper and send both sheets together through the printer.

3. Print out 6 copies each of units A and B of the 3″ block (on the pullout), with a $^1/_4$″ seam allowance added around the segments. Use these patterns to make 24 border blocks on point. You can get 2 copies of this size pattern on 1 sheet.

4. Print out 1 copy each of units A and B of the $4^1/_4$″ block (on the pullout), with a $^1/_4$″ seam allowance added around the segments. Use these patterns to make 4 corner blocks for the border.

Cutting the fabric

PURPLE

Center 6″ blocks: Cut 2 strips 4″ × the width of the fabric, then cut into 8 rectangles $7^3/_4$″ × 4″. Stack the rectangles so they are vertical with *right sides up.* Cut in half diagonally from the *lower left* corner to the *upper right* corner.

Tip

The large corner triangles are identical, so be sure to cut them with *all* right sides *up.*

Diagonal cut for rectangle, lower left to upper right

- Border 3″ blocks: Cut 3 strips $2^3/_4$″ × the width of the fabric, then cut 24 rectangles 5″ × $2^3/_4$″, positioning 2 layers of fabric with *wrong sides together.* Cut the rectangles in half diagonally. You should have 24 triangles oriented in 1 direction and 24 oriented in the opposite direction.

- Corner $4^1/_4$″ blocks: Cut 1 strip $3^1/_4$″ × the width of the fabric, then cut 4 rectangles 6″ × $3^1/_4$″. Stack the rectangles as pairs with *wrong sides together.* Cut these rectangles in half diagonally as you did for the border blocks.

- Binding: Cut 4 strips $2^1/_2$″ × the width of the fabric, then sew into 1 long strip.

MEDIUM BLUE

- Center 6″ blocks: Cut 2 strips 4″ × the width of the fabric. Cut these strips into 8 rectangles 7³/₄″ × 4″. Stack the rectangles so they are vertical with *right sides up*. Cut these rectangles in half diagonally from the *lower right* corner to the *upper left* corner (the opposite direction of the cut for the purple rectangles).

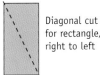

Diagonal cut for rectangle, right to left

LIGHT GOLD

- Center 6″ blocks: Cut 4 strips 2¹/₂″ × the width of the fabric. Do not subcut these strips.

- Border 3″ blocks and corner 4¹/₄″ blocks: Cut 4 strips 2″ × the width of the fabric. Do not subcut these strips.

- Setting triangles, sides: Cut 2 strips 5¹/₂″ × the width of the fabric. Cut these strips into 10 squares 5¹/₂″ × 5¹/₂″. Then cut these squares *diagonally twice* to make 40 triangles, each with the straight of grain on the longest side of the triangle.

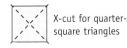

X-cut for quarter-square triangles

- Setting triangles, corners: Cut 1 strip 3⁷/₈″ × the width of the fabric. Cut this strip into 8 squares 3⁷/₈″ × 3⁷/₈″. Then cut these 8 squares diagonally to make 16 half-square triangles, with the straight of grain on 2 sides.

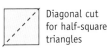

Diagonal cut for half-square triangles

Tip

Keep the setting triangles with the long straight-grain edge separate from those with two shorter straight-grain edges. They look very similar and could easily be confused during construction. Keeping the straight grain on the outer edge of the quilt is important to help prevent stretching.

DARK GOLD

- Center 6″ blocks: Cut 4 strips 2¹/₂″ × the width of the fabric. Do not subcut these strips.

- Border 3″ blocks and corner 4¹/₄″ blocks: Cut 4 strips 2″ × the width of the fabric. Do not subcut these strips.

- Inner border: Cut 4 strips 1¹/₄″ × the width of the fabric.

LIGHT RED

- Center 6″ blocks: Cut 1 strip 4¹/₂″ × the width of the fabric. Cut this strip into 8 squares 4¹/₂″ × 4¹/₂″. Cut these 8 squares diagonally to make 16 half-square triangles.

- Border 3″ blocks: Cut 1 strip 3″ × the width of the fabric. Cut this strip into 12 squares 3″ × 3″. Cut these 12 squares diagonally to make 24 half-square triangles.

- Corner 4¹/₄″ blocks: Cut 1 strip 3¹/₂″ × 7″. Cut this strip into 2 squares 3¹/₂″ × 3¹/₂″. Cut these 2 squares diagonally to make 4 half-square triangles.

DARK RED

Repeat the same cutting steps as for light red above.

Tip

Make a foil-wrapped pressing board to make pressing more efficient.

1. Wrap aluminum foil around 2 pieces of 8″ × 11″ mat board stacked together and insert into a tight-fitting fabric sleeve.

2. Use the board to iron your freezer-paper foundations to the fabric *from the paper side*. The reflected heat and the hard surface of the board work together to improve the sticking quality of the freezer paper. Do not use steam.

Piecing (for all blocks)

1. Place patch 1 right side down on the pressing board. The patch does not need to be cut perfectly since it will be trimmed along the way. Lay the freezer-paper pattern shiny side down on top of the patch, being careful to line up the longest side of the triangle patch 1 with the long edge of the fabric strip. The fabric strip you already cut on page 73 is large enough to cover the patch area with seam allowances all around.

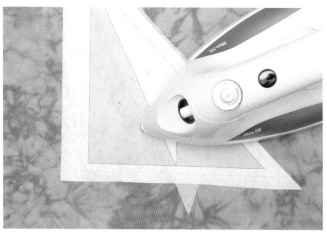

Iron first patch onto freezer-paper pattern

2. On the printed side of the freezer paper, line up the edge of the card-stock straightedge on the line between patches 1 and 2. Fold back the freezer paper along this line and carefully peel the *seam allowance* of patch 1 off the freezer paper. Trim the seam allowance of the patch to ¼″, using the Add-a-Quarter ruler and rotary cutter.

Foundation folded against card and seam allowance trimmed to ¼″

3. Line up patch 2 with patch 1, right sides together, matching the seam allowances. Be sure to position the fabric piece so it will cover the appropriate patch area on the pattern after it is sewn.

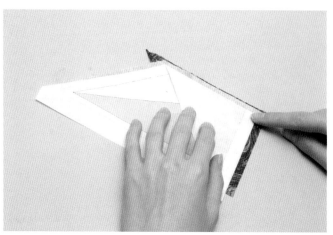

Line up seam allowances of patches 1 and 2.

4. Carefully sew this unit *next to the fold* of the foundation, using a regular stitch length. Do *not* sew through the paper.

Sewing *next to* the fold of the foundation

5. Flip out patch 2. You may want to press the seam allowance toward the darker fabric. If so, peel back the freezer-paper foundation just enough to finger-press the seam allowance of these 2 patches *toward patch 1*. Lay the freezer-paper foundation back over patch 2 and press from the paper side on the pressing board to adhere the fabric to the foundation.

This is one of the wonderful tricks you can do with freezer-paper foundations—you can control the direction of the seam allowance as you sew without disrupting the construction of the block.

6. For patch 3, continue as before.

7. Use the Add-a-Quarter ruler to trim the edge of the foundation unit on the outside dashed lines. Trim from the freezer-paper side. Carefully peel off the freezer-paper foundation. It can be reused!

Trimming edge of block

8. Repeat Steps 1–7 for the second unit of the block. Make sure the seam allowances are flipped in the opposite direction from those in the first unit.

9. Sew the 2 units together using a $1/4''$ seam and matching seam points in the center of the block. They should butt together easily.

10. Press the center diagonal seam allowance in the unit *open*. This will help reduce the bulk of seams when the blocks are pieced together.

Tip

I change the foundation after several uses because fabric lint sticks to the foundation and eventually it becomes less sticky. I can make at least 6 blocks from 1 foundation, and I can push a bit to get more than that. My record is 20 uses from 1 sheet.

Quilt assembly

CENTER

1. Piece 16 center blocks and decide which rotation you prefer—one of the illustrated versions, or one you create.

2. Sew the 16 center blocks together in rows of 4 each. Press the seams in alternate directions to distribute the bulk at the seam intersections. Sew the rows together. Press.

BORDERS

1. Add the inner border, using the $1^1/4''$ dark gold strips. Miter the corners.

2. Complete 24 of the 3″ blocks for the outer border.

3. Sew the quarter-square setting triangles to opposite sides of each block to create a diagonal unit. Be sure to use the triangles with the straight grain on the long side so the straight grain is on the outside edges of the border. Sew them together in groups of 6. Note that the first and last blocks in the border will need to have a half-square setting triangle added to 2 sides (see the assembly diagram). Press the seam allowances for each diagonal unit in opposite directions so the seam intersections will nest when the diagonal units are sewn together.

4. Make four $4^1/4''$ blocks for the corners, adding 1 to each end of top and bottom borders.

5. Assemble the quilt by sewing the side borders on first, then the longer top and bottom borders.

6. Layer, baste, quilt, and bind.

Assembly diagram

Anita Grossman Solomon

A completely novel way to use segmented foundations, involving both folding the foundation *and* stitching through it, was developed by Anita Grossman Solomon. Her methods eliminate much of the difficulty of matching points and lines when joining separate segments of blocks together.

Anita Grossman Solomon, from New York City, is an award-winning quilter and quilting instructor with a degree in art and a fresh perspective on the quiltmaking process. She invented "Make It Simpler" techniques to make quilting faster and easier and has written two books, contributed to magazines, and appeared on HGTV's *Simply Quilts*.

FOLDED ONE-PAGE FOUNDATIONS

I came across a bundle of scraps fifteen years ago and, with no quilting experience, I bought a sewing machine just to turn those scraps into a quilt. That sewing machine chewed up everything it came into contact with—except for some purchased Pineapple foundation papers. I looked into paper piecing and embraced the process, sewing oversized scraps to paper and trimming the excess away while at the machine. I had an early IBM computer—long before the sewing machine—and began churning out my own foundation patterns with Electric Quilt software as soon as it became available.

Thereafter, every block I made had at least one paper-pieced component. Every time I looked at a quilt or block, I analyzed it for "paper-pieceability." I even machine quilted my quilts by sewing through my paper patterns. I experimented with so many varieties of papers for foundations that they qualified as a stash on their own.

A few years ago, I was visualizing how to draw the foundation pattern for a block I had designed. Out of the blue, I realized that it was unnecessary to physically cut the block into four identical subunits for piecing. The foundation could be creased rather than cut, the subunits pieced on it, and then seamed together. Thus the idea for my "Make It Simpler" paper piecing was born. Since then, I have designed and published paper-piecing patterns for over 100 traditional blocks, simplifying both their construction and cutting. I never dreamed the day would come when I'd find it easier to construct a Pineapple block without a foundation and an unmarked ruler, but I have. I can't resist the urge to simplify quiltmaking techniques. I've taught weekly classes for seniors for twelve years and adapt techniques to suit them.

Spencer's Courthouse Steps (detail) by Anita Solomon, inspired by Lesly-Claire Greenberg's Log Cabin patterns, see full quilt on page 121.

Audition fabric choices

With this technique, quilt blocks are pieced entirely on one sheet of vellum that has been folded, rather than cut, into subunits. Since they were never cut apart, this means there are no separate subunits to join together.

I designed this block and my friend Susan Stauber made a full-sized quilt with an innovative layout, *Basement Constellation* on page 81. I suggest you construct a test block to learn the process. You'll then confidently cut more fabric and assembly-line sew several blocks into a larger project of your choice.

Sutton Star block

By Anita Grossman Solomon

Block size: 6″ × 6″

A scrap lover's dream, constructed with perfect points and intersections

Materials

FABRIC

Fabric for 1 block: small amounts of 6 different fabrics (The 4 ribbons will require only four 6″ × 1½″ strips of fabrics with contrasting values.)

OTHER SUPPLIES

- Translucent vellum paper (see Resources)
- Glue stick made specifically for fabric
- Clear packaging tape to reinforce templates
- Spray starch
- 6½″ square acrylic ruler
- Letter opener
- Optional: 2½″ square acrylic ruler
- Optional: Double-coated removable adhesive tape

Preparing the foundations

1. Make 2 photocopies of the pattern (on the pullout) on vellum. It is easier to make the necessary accurate folds with translucent vellum than with ordinary opaque paper.

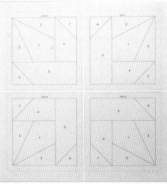

Creased pattern

2. Trim away the excess margin on 1 copy to ½″ beyond the outside dashed line. Fold the pattern between the dotted lines into quarters and crease. *Do not cut the pattern apart.* This is the foundation you will use to piece the block.

3. The Sutton Star is composed of 4 identical subunits. Photocopy the patterns (on the pullout) onto ordinary paper to make templates for cutting fabric pieces.

Note: Reinforce the templates by covering them, front and back, with a strip of clear packaging tape before cutting. I also position pieces of removable double-coated adhesive tape on the backs of the templates to prevent them from slipping while I am cutting the fabric.

Cutting the fabric

Starch the fabric to make the piecing and finger-pressing easier.

I precut the patches using templates to save time and use fabric economically. Cut several patches at once instead of trimming individual oversize patches once they've been sewn. A quarter-inch of fabric will extend over the seamline, which will serve as a guide to position the adjoining patch to be added, just as it would in conventional piecing.

- Template piece A is the "cone" shape.
- C and D are the "ribbons."
- B, its reverse (BR), and E are used for the background.

CONE SHAPES (A)

Stack fabric into 4 layers and use a $2^1/2''$ Omnigrid square to cut 4 squares. Position template A over the stack of squares, using it as a trimming guide to cut the squares into cones.

BACKGROUND SHAPES (B, BR, E)

1. Cut 4 B and 4 BR simultaneously. Lightly spray starch the wrong side of the fabric and press together. Cut pairs of $2^1/2''$ strips and use template B as a guide to cut through both layers, cutting B and BR (its reverse) at the same time. The B/BR patches have their sharp points blunted so the edges will align perfectly with the cone patches.

2. Cut 8 E. Cut 4 squares $1^7/8'' \times 1^7/8''$ and then cut them diagonally to make 8 triangles. Trim the triangles to the shape of template E.

RIBBON STRIPS

1. Cut 1 C and 1 D from each of 4 different starched fabrics. The ribbons will appear to weave in the center of the block if there is strong contrast between fabrics.

2. To quick-cut C and D ribbon patches, fold one $6'' \times 1^1/2''$ strip of fabric in half with wrong sides together. Lay template C on the strip with the blunted tip at the unfolded edge of the strip and trim away the triangles. Unfold the strip. Make a rotary cut across the strip at the straight end of C. You'll wind up with C, and the leftover piece will be D.

MAKING A MOCK-UP BLOCK

Use the second copy of the pattern to make a mock-up block by positioning the fabrics and patches right side up on the unprinted side of the unfolded copy. This will help keep the pieces in order and will allow you to see the effect of the fabrics in the finished block.

Piecing

Use a #14 needle and a shorter than usual stitch length.

Tip

The "one thread over" trick

When joining subunits and blocks, don't sew right on the line because the stitching takes up a bit of space and the block will end up slightly smaller than it should be. Instead, sew one thread-width over the line into the seam allowance. When piecing subunits (say, sewing piece 2 to piece 1), there is no seam allowance for you to sew "one thread over" into. Instead, sew one thread over into the area that is not yet covered by fabric (the area 2 is to occupy).

1. Take the A patches (the cones) from the mock-up and lightly glue each, right side up, to the unprinted side of the folded foundation in position 1. Each patch should extend $1/4''$ from all edges of the cone pattern stitching line, creating the $1/4''$ seam allowance. I use a fabric glue stick rather than pins. This glue is safe for fabric and separates easily from the vellum when the time comes.

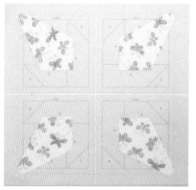

Four A patches in place

Tip

When adding the #1 patches to the vellum foundation paper, lightly apply the glue stick to the unprinted side of the foundation. Lay the patch *wrong side up* on a work surface. If the patch is light in color, lay it on a dark surface, and vice versa. It is much simpler to bring the foundation to the patch than trying to position the patch onto the foundation.

2. Glue, rather than pin or hold, all 4 B patches into position for sewing patch 2. Turn the foundation paper over and sew all patches.

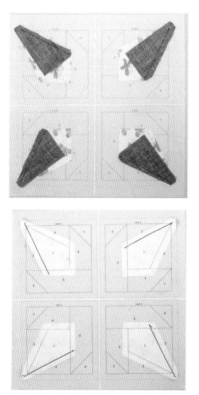

B patches glued and then sewn in place

Tip

Place the patch to be added, right side up, onto scrap paper and apply glue to the seam allowance. Any excess glue will land on the paper. The glue should not extend beyond the seam allowance.

3. Press the B patches open. Add the BR patches and stitch and open them. If the patches won't lie flat on the foundation, glue them down, either to the paper or A to B, within their seam allowances. This will keep them from flipping out of place during future rounds of sewing.

B and BR patches sewn and opened

4. Repeat the process for the remaining patches, following the numeric piecing order. Note that the 8 small background E triangles can be glued into place at one time before sewing.

All fabric pieces sewn in place on subunits

Assembly

Since the block's subunits were never separated, it is a simple matter to join them at the seamlines.

1. Trim away any fabric extending over a fold line. Refold the foundation block, encasing the fabric, along either 1 of the 2 previously creased long lines running through the center. If you forgot to fold and crease the foundation prior to piecing, all is not lost. Stitch through the fold line with an unthreaded sewing machine needle to needlepunch the foundation.

2. Begin sewing at the top of the block, through the seam allowance and along the printed sewing line. Stop sewing where the line ends for the first subunit. Clip the thread and hop over the interior seam allowances, beginning to sew again on the remaining sewing line; sew beyond the outside edge of the block.

3. Make a perpendicular clip at least ³/₈″ through the center of the foundation at the fold line.

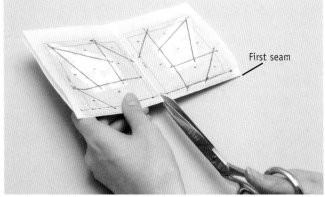

First seam

First seam sewn, then a clip through the center

4. Fold the foundation perpendicular to the sewn seam, fabric sides together.

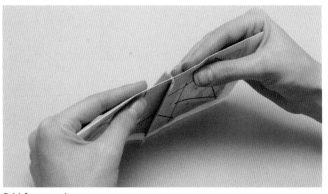

Fold for second seam

5. Sew this side of the block together as before, but do not sew the upper and lower flaps to the foundation. Clip the threads and backstitch at the center of the foundation after moving the flaps out of the way.

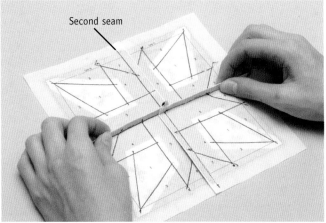

Second seam

Second seam sewn

6. Press the block with the seams running clockwise. Because the block's center seam allowances are unsewn, the seams can be manipulated in any direction you wish. Use a letter opener to slit the paper at the folds and remove the folded paper in the seam allowances.

7. Trim the block to 6¹/₂″ × 6¹/₂″, matching the center of the block, from the back, with the center of a 6¹/₂″ square ruler. Do not rely on the printed edge of the foundation as a trimming guide since it's likely the paper will have shrunk during the block's construction.

You won't be able to tell that the block was pieced with my technique. After all, the technique is just a means to an end, and it will be your personality that flavors the block.

You can use this design for a bigger project:

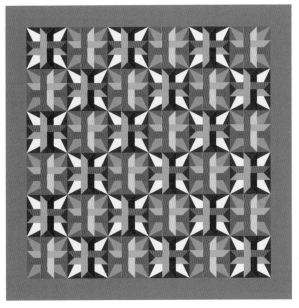

Sutton Star, made with 2 colorways. Fabric requirements for this small quilt of 36 blocks: $5/8$ yard each of 2 colors for A (cones); $7/8$ yard each of 2 colors for B, BR, and E (background); $3/8$ yard each of 8 fabrics for ribbon patches; and 1 yard for the border.

Basement Constellation by Susan Stauber. This quilt contains 224 blocks, each sashed with black, set in a horizontal half drop. It is made with scraps for the Sutton Star blocks, with many C and D patches cut individually to create special effects and to control the contrast where fabrics meet. Photo by Sharon Risedorph.

CHAPTER SIX

Piecing With Strips

Quiltmakers have used strips to make quilt designs for years. String piecing was especially popular during the late nineteenth and early twentieth century when scraps and selvedge strips were sewn to each other on top of paper foundations. Strips were pieced horizontally, vertically, or diagonally, on whole blocks as well as on shapes such as diamonds or triangles, which were then pieced into block designs.

Foundations can certainly stabilize strips, which tend to wobble and stretch, and we'll show you two different ways to do this. In the first one, Peggy Martin has taken strip piecing to a new and clever level by using measured straight strips to piece complex designs with shapes that do *not* finish as strips but as points and asymmetric shapes. By working on foundations, of course, she has absolute control of the pieces.

Peggy Martin

Peggy Martin, from San Diego, California, has been teaching and lecturing since 1988. She has developed her own quick and accurate techniques, including a strip assembly-line approach to foundation piecing. She has written two books about her quick-strip technique.

QUICK-STRIP PAPER PIECING

I learned to sew when I was eight years old and made most of my own clothing for years. In 1981 I took my first quilting class. It was taught in the most traditional way: templates were used for all shapes, each shape was drawn around, and the sewing line was drawn for hand piecing. I enjoyed the process but was frustrated by how long it took to finish even one block, much less a whole quilt top! And, of course, we wouldn't even consider machine quilting in those days—everything was hand quilted as well.

A few years later, rotary cutters, new rulers, and faster methods of cutting and sewing were being developed for machine piecing. It was easy to cut strips with a rotary cutter, and many quilts were adapted for faster, assembly-line methods using strips or shapes cut from strips. I was definitely a convert to faster, more efficient methods because they made quilting so much more fun, with much quicker results.

I have always loved the design possibilities of foundation piecing, but I often found the process to be slow and time-consuming. When I first learned foundation paper piecing around 1990, I was told just to "cut a piece a little bigger than you need." I was used to cutting strips from my fabrics for other projects, so I did the same thing when foundation piecing. Cutting a strip left a much cleaner piece of yardage than just cutting chunks out randomly, and using a strip for the foundations also helped make sure I didn't end up with a piece that was too short to cover the area.

When I began sewing and designing blocks that had multiple units that were the same, I sewed them all at one time along the strip—just as you would sew an assembly-line Log Cabin quilt. Suddenly, paper piecing was much faster, more fun, and more mistake-proof! My students loved this new method because it was so much faster and more accurate, and beginning paper piecers found it an easy way to learn foundation piecing.

My method is called "quick-strip paper piecing" and, quite simply, it uses strips for each area on the pattern.

New York Beauty (detail) by Peggy Martin, see full quilt on page 120.

Repeat units are pieced all at the same time along the strip, making the process amazingly fast.

When sewing the blocks, keep the following in mind:

- Always keep the seam allowance consistently to the *right* side of the needle (just as we normally sew a seam).

- Arrows on the pattern always point *toward the sewing machine* (away from you) to help you orient the pattern correctly on the strip.

- Large bold numbers on the pattern indicate the order in which the strips will be sewn.

- Smaller numbers on the pattern indicate the width to cut the strip for that piece.

By following these guidelines and the step-by-step directions below, you'll be well on your way to faster foundation piecing with fewer mistakes and less wasted fabric.

Star Swept

By Peggy Martin

Quilt size: 37″ × 37″
Block size: 6″ × 6″

Materials

FABRIC

- Dark purple: 1 yard
- Turquoise and green print: $\frac{1}{4}$ yard
- Medium green: $\frac{3}{8}$ yard
- Light green and purple batik: $\frac{5}{8}$ yard
- Green and purple print: $\frac{1}{2}$ yard
- Turquoise stripe: $\frac{1}{4}$ yard
- Large green, turquoise, and purple print: $\frac{5}{8}$ yard
- Backing: $1\frac{1}{4}$ yards
- Batting: 42″ × 42″

This vibrant wall quilt goes together quickly and easily using the quick-strip paper-piecing technique.

OTHER SUPPLIES

- Foundation material (I prefer 18- to 20-pound photocopy paper.)
- Spray starch
- Open-toe presser foot for sewing machine

Preparing the foundations

Make 32 copies of the Star Swept pattern on page 88.

Tip

To save paper, make 2 copies of the pattern and tape them to 1 sheet of paper. Then make 15 more copies and cut out the 32 patterns on the outer dashed line.

Cutting the strips

Tip

Spray starch and iron the fabrics before cutting them to help stabilize and prevent distortion of the fabric. All strips are cut from selvedge to selvedge.

CENTER BLOCKS (MAKE 8 PATTERN UNITS, FOR 4 BLOCKS)

Note: All numbers below (#1, #3, etc.) refer to areas on the Star Swept pattern.

- Dark purple: Cut 3 strips $2^{1}/_{4}''$ × the width of the fabric for #1, #3, and #5.

- Turquoise and green print: Cut 1 strip $2^{1}/_{4}''$ × the width of the fabric for #2; cut 1 strip $2''$ × the width of the fabric for #4.

- Medium green: Cut 1 strip $1^{3}/_{4}''$ × the width of the fabric for #6.

SURROUNDING BLOCKS (MAKE 24 PATTERN UNITS, FOR 12 BLOCKS)

- Light green and purple batik: Cut 8 strips $2^{1}/_{4}''$ × the width of the fabric for #1, #3, and #5.

- Green and purple print: Cut 3 strips $2^{1}/_{4}''$ × the width of the fabric for #2; cut 3 strips $2''$ × the width of the fabric for #4.

- Turquoise stripe: Cut 3 strips $1^{3}/_{4}''$ × the width of the fabric for #6.

SETTING TRIANGLES

- Dark purple: Cut 1 strip $4^{1}/_{2}''$ × the width of the fabric; cut into 8 squares $4^{1}/_{2}'' \times 4^{1}/_{2}''$, then cut once on the diagonal for 16 triangles for the center block and surrounding block corners.

BORDERS

- Dark purple (for 1st border): Cut 4 strips $2''$ × the width of the fabric; cut into 2 strips $2'' \times 24^{1}/_{2}''$ and 2 strips $2'' \times 27^{1}/_{2}''$.

- Medium green (for 2nd border): Cut 4 strips $1^{1}/_{2}''$ × the width of the fabric; cut into 2 strips $1^{1}/_{2}'' \times 27^{1}/_{2}''$ and 2 strips $1^{1}/_{2}'' \times 29^{1}/_{2}''$.

- Large green, turquoise, and purple print (for 3rd border): Cut 4 strips $4^{1}/_{2}''$ × the width of the fabric; cut into 2 strips $4^{1}/_{2}'' \times 29^{1}/_{2}''$ and 2 strips $4^{1}/_{2}'' \times 37^{1}/_{2}''$.

BINDING

- Dark purple: Cut 4 strips $2''$ × the width of the fabric.

Sewing the units

Tip

If you have an extension table or sewing cabinet for your sewing machine, it will make positioning your patterns on the strips much easier!

1. Begin with the center block units. Place the strip for #1 (dark purple) right sides together *on top of* strip 2 (turquoise/green print), with the right edges aligned. Lay the strips on your sewing machine throat plate, just as if you were going to sew a $^{1}/_{4}''$ seam on the right side. Find the line on the pattern you will be sewing, between areas 1 and 2. Position the pattern so that area 1 is to the left and area 2 is to the right. The arrows in 1 and 2 will both point away from you, toward the sewing machine. Lay the sewing line of the paper on the $^{1}/_{4}''$ seamline of the fabric. With an open-toe presser foot and stitches set to 16–18 per inch (1.75 metric), sew along the first line of the first pattern unit.

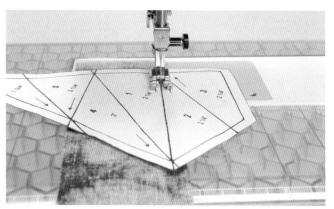

Sewing the first line

2. Position and sew the remaining 7 pattern units on the strip in exactly the same way. (Check the strips often to make sure they stay aligned and don't drift apart as you sew the units.)

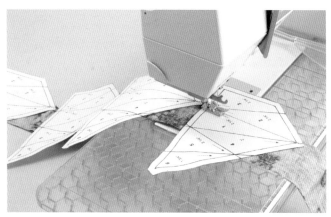

Sewing the first line on 8 units

3. Cut the threads and remove the sewn strip from the sewing machine. With the paper patterns on top, reach under and open out fabric strip 2 from strip 1. You do not need to press yet. Roughly cut apart the units with scissors.

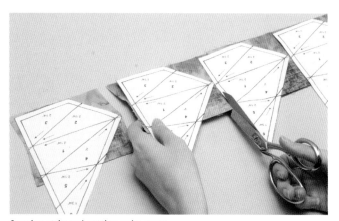

Opening strip and cutting units apart

4. To press the units, set your iron to a dry setting and place a piece of muslin or other light fabric on the ironing surface to prevent any ink transfer from the patterns. Press the 8 units on the fabric side by opening out strip 2 with the iron, making sure the inked paper side is on the protected ironing surface. Loosely trim away any fabric that extends beyond the outside edges of the paper. (You don't need to trim exactly yet—just trim close to the edge of the paper.)

5. Lay strip 3 (dark purple) *right side up* on the throat plate, again as if you were going to sew a ¹/₄″ seam on the right side. Position the paper pattern so the line between areas 2 and 3 is where the ¹/₄″ sewing line on the fabric will be, and the arrow in area 3 is pointing toward the sewing machine (area 3 will be to the right of area 2). Sew on the line and lay the remaining 7 units on the strip in the same way, butting the units up as you did in Step 1. It is all right to overlap the paper patterns in areas that are not part of the seam.

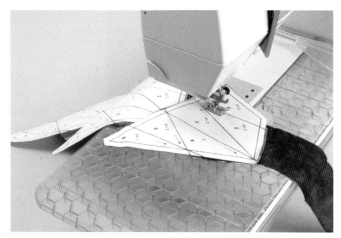

Sewing strip 3

6. Open out fabric strip 3 and, with the paper patterns on top, cut the units apart, taking care not to cut through the paper or to cut the fabric under area 3 too short. There is extra fabric in the seam allowance from the previous strip, and this needs to be trimmed before pressing. With the fabric side of the unit toward you, fold the paper under and crease it along the seamline just sewn. Trim the seam allowance to ¹/₄″ for all 8 units.

Trimming excess seam allowance

7. Fold the paper back so the pattern is flat, open out the fabric of strip 3, and press as before. Trim away any fabric that extends beyond the outside edges of the paper.

8. For the remaining strips, repeat Steps 3 and 4, referring to Cutting the Strips on page 85 for the correct strip for each area. (Note that you will be turning the pattern around to piece areas 4, 5, and 6 to keep the arrow in each area pointing toward the sewing machine.) Make 8 units for the 4 center blocks. After all units are sewn and pressed, trim the outer edges cleanly along the outer seamline using your rotary cutter and ruler.

Center pattern unit; make 8

9. If you desire, the paper can be removed now to make the block assembly less bulky. (The paper can be left in until your top is completely assembled if it makes you more comfortable.) Remove the paper in the reverse order that the seams were sewn. On a table or other hard surface, fold the paper back and crease it along the seamline, then tear the paper away while

supporting the seam and fabric with your other hand. Handle the pieces carefully to prevent stretching.

10. Piece the remaining 24 units for the surrounding blocks in the same manner, using the strips as outlined in the cutting list. You can piece all 24 units at 1 time along the strips, or you might choose to do 8 units at a time—a total of 3 times.

Surrounding block units; make 24

Assembly

1. Sew the center units into 4 pairs. Press the seams to 1 side. Add a setting triangle to the corner of each pair and press toward the triangle. The triangles are slightly oversized, so trim up the corner to make the block 6$\frac{1}{2}$˝ square after pressing.

Center blocks (pattern units sewn in pairs with setting triangle added and squared up)

2. Assemble the 24 surrounding block units into 12 pairs. Add a setting triangle to each pair as in Step 1.

Surrounding blocks (pattern units sewn in pairs with setting triangle added and squared up)

3. Lay out the blocks as shown in the assembly diagram and sew the squares together in rows. Sew the rows together and add the 3 borders, 1 at a time.

4. If you did not remove the paper before assembly, remove it now, again removing the paper in the reverse order that the seams were sewn. (This would be the outer border seams first, the seams joining the blocks, then #6, #5, etc.) Baste and quilt as you desire. I quilted my *Star Swept* quilt by machine with lots of swirls and spirals to add to the motion of the quilt. Bind and sew a label on the back.

Assembly diagram

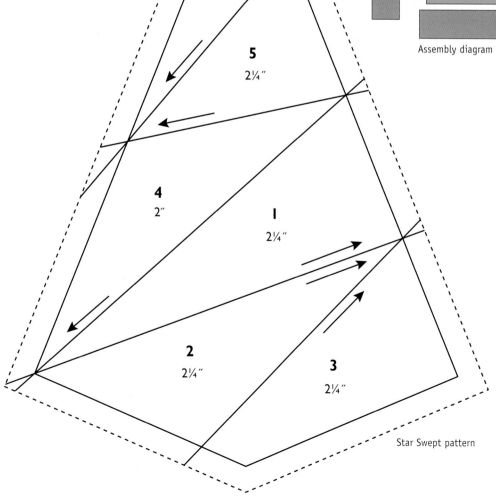

6
1¾″

5
2¼″

4
2″

1
2¼″

2
2¼″

3
2¼″

Star Swept pattern

CLASSIC STRIP PIECING

Peggy Martin's quick-strip method of foundation piecing uses measured straight strips of fabric to piece sharp points with angled sides in segments within the block. For straight strips sewn parallel to each other, an alternative is to sew the fabric strips together first, making a large piece of fabric from which to cut segments.

This is the quick-piecing method Barbara Johannah pioneered 30 years ago, streamlining the traditional piecing process. Long strips of fabric are sewn together into strip sets, which are then cut into shapes to create quilt patterns. Quilters accepted this idea quickly, constructing entire quilt tops without having to cut and sew individual patches. This happened at a time when the quilt revival was beginning to pick up speed, and quilters were hungry for new ideas.

I have used quick-piecing for many traditional patterns. Sometimes the long lines of stitching for the strip sets were a little wobbly, sometimes the fabric stretched, and sometimes the segments didn't always fit together exactly as I had planned. When I tried *under* pressed piecing strip sets on a freezer-paper foundation, I discovered that I ended up with segments that were identical, and the final match points did not vary.

Working this way does add some time to quick-piecing, both in preparation and stitching. But the resulting accuracy makes it a great technique to use, whether you are making a simple Rail Fence, a complicated Lone Star, or an off-the-wall op art design.

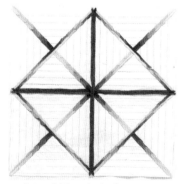

Mock Log Cabin unit, back

Mock Log Cabin

By Jane Hall

Quilt size: 18″ × 18″
Block size: 9″ × 9″

This graphic design is quickly, easily, and accurately pieced using strip sets on foundations. This graphic design is quickly, easily, and accurately pieced using strip sets on foundations.

Materials

FABRIC

¼ yard each of 6 coordinating fabrics, graded from light to dark (These can be prints, hand-dyes, or batiks, in yardage or fat quarters.)

OTHER SUPPLIES

- Freezer paper
- Template material or large triangle ruler (at least 9″)

Preparing the foundations

Freezer paper is firm and durable and will keep long strips and segments straight through a lot of handling. Gridded freezer paper has measured lines already printed on it. It is not difficult, however, to draw your own lines on ordinary grocery-store freezer paper, which offers the advantage of unlimited length.

You will need several long strip sets from which to cut 16 triangles. Cut 2 foundations 5˝ × 38˝ long (for 6 triangles each) and 1 piece 5˝ × 26˝ long (for the remaining 4 triangles). If you are working with fat quarters, you will need 5 foundations 5˝ × 21˝ and 1 foundation 5˝ × 11˝.

1. Draw 7 long parallel lines on the dull side of the freezer paper, ³⁄₄˝ apart, to make a total of 6 spaces, taking care to make these lines and spaces exact. Add ¹⁄₄˝ for the seam allowance outside the top and bottom space. With long skinny strips, I prefer having the seam allowance *included* in the foundation for stability, even though it is tiresome to pick the paper out later.

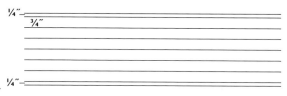

Draw parallel lines on freezer paper.

2. Make a template for the triangle pattern (on the pullout), or study the ruler to find the exact lines for a 9˝ triangle.

3. Trace the triangle pattern onto the dull side of the foundations 16 times, matching the piecing lines and dovetailing the shapes. Place 1 up and 1 down, as shown in the diagram. It is important to place the top point of each triangle exactly at the outer line of the foundation each time. Position the shapes on the foundation at least ³⁄₄˝ apart horizontally, to allow for ¹⁄₄˝ seam allowances. Do **not** cut triangles apart yet.

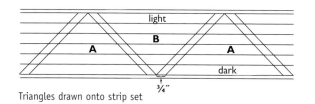

Triangles drawn onto strip set

4. Make 8 A triangles with dark outer strips, and 8 B triangles with light outer strips. If you have been able to trace an equal number of A and B triangles on all the strip-set foundations, you will have the right

number of each. If not, change the positioning of the triangles as needed to obtain 8 of each. Labeling the foundations is helpful.

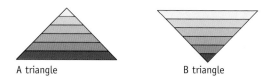

A triangle   B triangle

Cutting the fabric

From each of the 6 fabrics, cut 3 strips 1¹⁄₄˝ × the width of the fabric. (If using fat quarters, cut 6 strips 1¹⁄₄˝ × the width of the fat quarter.)

Piecing

The strip sets will be pieced identically in gradations from dark to light. If you begin piecing each strip set with the same value fabric, matching the seams will be easier because the seam allowances will usually face in opposite directions so the segments can be nested.

1. Lay a strip of the darkest fabric on the ironing board, right side down. Position the freezer paper foundation on top of the strip, shiny side against the fabric, matching the cut edge of the fabric to one long edge of the paper. The opposite long edge of the strip should overlap the next line drawn on the foundation by ¹⁄₄˝. Press carefully on the dull side of the paper, but only over the area where the fabric strip is placed.

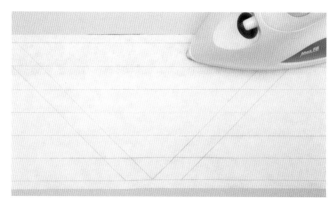

Ironing the foundation onto the first strip

2. Lay the second strip on top of the first one, right sides together, matching the cut edges of the fabrics. Pin occasionally down the length of the fabric to keep the strips aligned, placing the pins well away from the sewing line.

Second strip pinned in place

3. Turn the foundation over, with the fabric against the feed dogs, and stitch on the second line in from the edge of the foundation. Use a slightly smaller than usual stitch: 16–18 stitches per inch, or 1.75 metric.

Sewing on the line

4. Finger-press the added strip open and iron it to the foundation, taking care not to touch the iron to the exposed shiny part of the freezer paper. I dart in with the tip of my iron and touch the fabric to anchor it. Then I use the side of the iron and press firmly from the seam out toward the loose edge to make sure no excess fabric forms a fold at the seamline. When strip piecing on a foundation, it is important to press well to ensure accurate segments. It's especially vital not to trap a fold onto the freezer paper. As you add strips, pressing gets easier since you have covered more of the foundation.

Pressing the strip

5. Continue adding strips in order, pinning, stitching, and pressing each strip. Check that each seam allowance is ample but *not too wide*. A scant $1/4''$ is perfect. Since you are sewing "upside down" and not looking at the fabric, the long skinny strips can wobble slightly, making the free edge uneven. Folding the foundation and trimming is an option, but I find it easy to position each new strip by gauging its distance from already sewn seams. If there is any doubt about where the seamline is, I stab a couple of pins through the drawn line to the back to make sure I am in the right place. Trim after stitching if you haven't done so before.

6. When the foundation is completely covered, give a final press to the strip set to make sure that all the fabric sticks to the foundation. I press from both the fabric side and the foundation side.

Pressing finished strip set

7. Piece the second strip set in the same way. Cut out the triangles, adding a ¼″ seam allowance on all sides. You should have 8 A triangles (begin with the lightest fabric at the point and end with the darkest) and 8 B triangles that are the reverse.

8. At this point, press the cut edges of the triangles one more time. Freezer paper sticks well to fabric but can loosen with handling, and the edges need to stick tightly to the foundations.

Assembling the block

1. Lay out the triangles in the pattern of your choice, with either a dark or a light center.

Assembly layout options for triangle segments

2. Match 2 A triangles together so that the angled lines as well as the stitching lines meet exactly. Pin the short sides together, matching intersections and beginning and ending points.

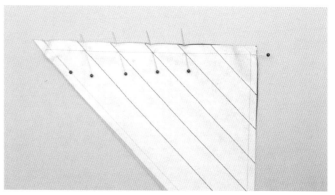

Segments pinned together

Tip

Before sewing, double-check the intersections. Fold open the seam allowance after you have stabbed a pin through the intersection and check that the two opposing seams meet in a perfect line. If need be, adjust them so the seams meet. Then pin vertically, and stitch slowly, withdrawing the pins as you come to them. With angled lines, you may need to work to pinpoint the exact place they cross. For these particular segments, where the lines meet horizontally, it is a simple matter to position them exactly, then pin and sew.

Checking the intersection match

3. Open out the triangles and check the intersections. The seams should match. If the pressure of your presser foot has pushed them slightly off, it is very easy to remove stitching about ½″ on either side of the offending place. Re-pin and then resew, running

the seam under the machine from a different direction (so the pressure is applied differently).

4. Pin and stitch the remaining pairs of A triangles together. Repeat to make 4 pairs of B triangles. Remove the foundation from the joining seam allowances (a picky job!) and press the seams open so you don't lose the accuracy you've worked so hard to get. You will have 8 sets of double triangles.

5. Join an A double triangle to a B double triangle along the long sides, making a square. As before, pin all intersections and make sure the centerlines are exact. Remove the foundations from the seam allowances and press the seams open. Rotate each square 90° to create the illusion of a square on top of a square, in the design of your choice.

6. Join the 4 squares. These seams are easy since there aren't any cross-seams or intersections within them. Do take care that the center seams, both horizontal and diagonal, match exactly.

This 16-triangle unit can be replicated to create a graphic bed quilt, or finished as is to make a wall hanging, perhaps with an added border. Wait to remove the foundation paper from the piece until all blocks are joined and the piece has at least one border surrounding it. You worked hard to keep these strips stabilized, so you don't want to eliminate the paper that is keeping everything straight and even.

Two more strip-pieced designs using basically the same triangle as *Mock Log Cabin* are *End of the Day* and *Op Art*.

Don't stop here. If you are an aficionado of strip piecing, think about using foundations for other patterns, simple or complicated. Checkerboards, string patterns, and bargello designs all work well for strip-pieced borders, pieced on freezer paper to control the final measurement. If you have yearned to make some of the fabulous op art designs with swooping lines and strong black-and-white contrast, consider making them with foundations. The control and precision you can achieve are incredible—all without having to worry about sewing an exact $1/4$″ seam allowance.

Tip

For tiny strips and vertical slices in a strip set, as in a bargello design, press piece the cut slices together onto a foundation with lines drawn for the joining seams. This guarantees that the final piece will be true to size, even with long, thin, stretchy, wobbly parts.

Op Art quilt (detail): triangles separated by small center segments with reverse values, see full quilt on page 123.

End of the Day quilt: triangles positioned vertically on the strip set

CHAPTER SEVEN

SINGLE TEMPLATE
Piecing

Single template piecing is a departure from pressed-piecing techniques. Every piece in the block has its own foundation, which is not sewn *on* but sewn *with*. The foundations are templates, one for each patch in the block, and they remain on the patches during construction. The template edges are the guide for stitching the patches together. As with pressed piecing, the foundations stabilize the piecing and provide exceptional precision.

This technique is a direct descendent of English paper piecing, a valued technique that has been in use for several hundred years. Seam allowances are basted over templates to produce finished shapes, which are then hand whipped together. The accuracy is incredible since lines and finished points match directly. The amount of time it takes is equally incredible.

In current practice, you make a freezer-paper pattern, cut the pieces apart, press the pieces onto fabric, trim the fabric $1/4''$ larger than the templates, and sew the pieces together to re-create the original paper pattern in fabric. It is simple to pair and pin patches together, then stitch exactly at the edge of the paper template by hand or by machine. The paper stays on through the whole process (although curved seams require a slightly different technique).

Ruth B. McDowell

Ruth B. McDowell has successfully used this technique for a number of years. Her incredible fabric choices and her artful work with nature subjects are known worldwide. She is not a fan of traditional pressed piecing but makes skillful use of this form of template piecing.

Ruth B. McDowell, of Winchester, Massachusetts, has made about 400 pieced art quilts and has lectured and taught design workshops worldwide for 25 years. Her art quilts are included in many private, corporate, and museum collections, and two of her quilts were included in *The Twentieth Century's Best American Quilts*. She is the author of eight books.

TEMPLATE FOUNDATION PIECING

My art quilts are all assembled by machine piecing, right sides together, in the old-fashioned way. I find that this style of piecing gives an integrity to the surface that I can't get with other assembly methods. It forces a degree of abstraction in the design, which I enjoy. It also integrates the elements of the quilt in a unique way, as the construction process becomes part of the design.

Over time, I have adapted a traditional approach to templates to create my current method. It allows me to control a number of different decisions that I find crucial for my kind of art.

It is absolutely necessary for me to be able to audition each and every fabric piece, cut to size, with all the other pieces before I start to sew. Many different subtleties in color, value, and pattern can only be perceived with the actual fabrics next to each other. I use a huge

Leaves of Another Year (detail) by Ruth B. McDowell. See full quilt on page 124. Photo by David Caras.

range of different kinds of cotton fabrics from many different sources in each quilt. Which one is the right one depends on a lot of issues, including being able to see what the fabric pieces look like in context—that is, all cut and placed as they will be in the quilt. Then I can change those I'm not happy with and try others. I spend at least as much time on the choices of the background pieces as I do on the subject.

With my method, the freezer-paper template is ironed to the *back* of the fabric piece, and a seam allowance is added around the edge of the paper. The fabric piece (with the paper template on the back) can be pinned on the design to audition the fabrics before sewing begins. Changes are easily made by peeling the paper off the first fabric and re-ironing it to a different fabric. This can be done several times if necessary.

The paper edge becomes a guide in sewing the seam. I don't sew through the paper, so it is easier to remove at the end of the piecing.

This method also allows me to work from a full-size drawing of the quilt, in which each line is a seamline. In the instructions for my project, you will see that I have come up with a tactic that doesn't reverse the original image in the way that many other methods that use freezer-paper templates do.

Pressing the seam allowance to one side or the other makes a huge difference in the look of a pieced quilt. It's exactly the same difference that an appliqué artist takes into account in choosing whether to appliqué or reverse appliqué an element. The seam allowance will pad one side of a seamline, making the piece it is pressed under appear to come forward. For instance, I will press a seam allowance under a branch piece and away from a sky piece to make the branch come forward and the sky recede. Where two pieces should appear on the same plane—for example, a reflection on the surface of water—the seam might be pressed *open*.

I need a method that gives a high degree of accuracy. It must also allow for complicated patterns of seaming and for curved seams as well as straight or angled seams. I developed a system for the tightest practical pieced curved seam and for accurately assembling designs with multiple curves to give me greater freedom in design. Many other curved seam methods are only practical for gentle curves.

I have used this method for more than ten years—in my art quilts, in my books, and in classes with hundreds of students. With straight seams, my method is easily taught to beginners, and they have successfully pieced many apparently complicated quilts. Curved seams require a lot more patience and skill, but with careful attention they can be taught to slightly more experienced sewers.

My small project is an abstract tree. Most of the tree is created with straight seams, but I've included a few curved seams as well. It is a pattern that will reward careful auditioning of fabrics and attention to the pressing of seam allowances, and it will provide an introduction to straight seam piecing and some elegant curves.

Abstract Tree

By Ruth B. McDowell

Quilt size: $11^{1}/_{4}$″ × $14^{3}/_{4}$″
Block size: $7^{1}/_{4}$″ × $9^{3}/_{4}$″

Note: This block was designed to demonstrate various unique aspects of my freezer-paper template process. It is sewable at the size it appears in this book. You may enjoy the process more, however, if you double the size of the block on a copier to $14^{1}/_{2}$″ × $19^{1}/_{2}$″. You will also need to increase the border and backing yardage accordingly.

Materials

FABRIC
- Tree and background: small amounts of fabric with various selections to try
- Sky: a variety of patterns in related colors (not just one fabric)
- Border: $^{1}/_{4}$ yard
- Backing: $^{1}/_{2}$ yard
- Batting: 15″ × 19″
- Binding: $^{1}/_{4}$ yard

OTHER SUPPLIES
- Freezer paper for foundations
- Permanent marker (extra-fine or ultra-fine Sharpie)
- Artist's colored pencils (*not* watercolor pencils)

Preparing the foundations

1. Make a copy of the block pattern (on the pullout) on the *shiny* side of freezer paper, using a fine permanent marker. This will counter the mirror image effect since the fabric will be placed on the same side as the drawn lines. Copy only the seamlines, not the labels on the pieces.

Tip

If you are using very light-colored fabrics, a bit of the marker seamlines may transfer to the wrong side of the fabric along the seamline. If this bothers you, use a hard pencil instead of a marker.

2. Turn the freezer paper over, dull side up. You will be able to see the seamlines you just drew through the freezer paper if you place it on a light-colored table or a white sheet of paper. With a colored pencil or highlighter, draw a grain line on the *dull side* of the freezer paper just *inside* the outside edge of the quilt pattern.

Abstract Tree. This block, which requires careful fabric choices, uses a system that works for both straight and curved seam piecing.

Draw grain line at outside edge of pattern.

3. Using a pencil, add tick marks on the *dull side* of the freezer paper to help in matching the seams during piecing; make ticks at intersections and 1″–2″ apart along the seams. Use different colors of pencils or different symbols as ticks as an aid in matching the right pieces. Mark the star on the big curve as shown, for final assembly of the quilt.

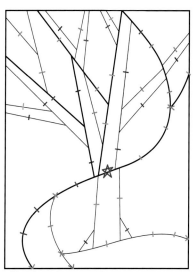

Add tick marks to templates.

4. Use a colored pencil to mark the section lines (the darker lines on the block diagram) on the dull side of the freezer paper. The section lines divide the block into sewable units. Label the sections.

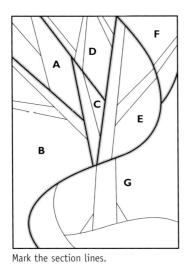

Mark the section lines.

Label the individual pieces as well, to keep track of the templates.

5. Lay the printed block diagram on a table or pin it to a design wall to use as a guide.

6. Cut the freezer-paper pattern apart on the section lines, cutting the templates apart as you use them rather than cutting them all at once.

Selecting and cutting the fabric

1. Select fabrics for your block. In this case, I used a single fabric for all the pieces of the tree. Lay out fabrics or pin pieces to the block diagram to help you audition the choices.

When cutting the pieces of fabric for your block, put the colored grain line (drawn in Step 2) on grain (lined up with the threads in the cloth). Having the pieces of fabric on the outside of the block on grain will help keep your block square. It doesn't matter which way you place the paper templates without the colored grain line on the fabric because the pieces are inside the block.

If you want to use a fabric with stripes in a certain way—like the streaky fabric I used for the tree branches in this sample—place the templates to line up with the stripes rather than the grain line. Be aware that those pieces will have a bias edge on the outside of the block and handle them carefully.

2. When you have decided which fabric to use, *place the freezer-paper template pieces SHINY SIDE DOWN on the BACK of the fabric.* Leave room around each piece, placing them at least 1/2″ apart, as you will need to add a seam allowance outside the freezer-paper template.

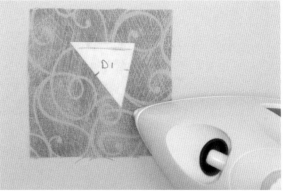

Freezer-paper template ironed onto back of fabric

Tip

Use the cotton setting on your iron, with steam, to iron the freezer paper to the wrong side of the selected fabric. The plastic (shiny) coating on the freezer paper will adhere it temporarily to the back of the fabric. The use of steam helps it to stick. If you have trouble with the paper falling off too easily, the iron is not hot enough.

3. Cut out the fabric pieces. For straight seams, align the 1/4″ line of a clear plastic ruler with the edge of the freezer-paper templates. Cut along the ruler's edge, with 1/4″ seam allowances, with a rotary cutter.

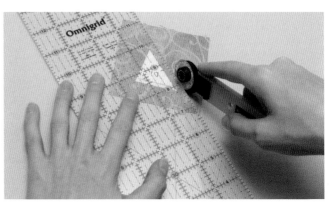

Cutting straight pieces

4. For the curved seams, cut the ¼″ seam allowances carefully by eye with scissors.

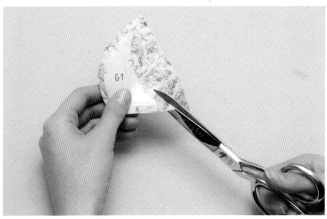

Cutting curved seam by eye

5. For the curved seams, trace a line on the fabric along all the curved edges of the freezer-paper templates, both concave (inward curved) and convex (outward curved), with a standard colored pencil (not a chalk or watercolor pencil) to mark the seamline. Place the tick marks along the curves in the seam allowances. Clip the seam allowances on the concave edges.

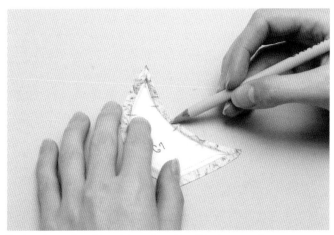

Tracing along edge of template and marking ticks in seam allowance

As you cut each piece of fabric, lay or pin it in place on the pattern block diagram to check your fabric choices. The seam allowances will overlap slightly, but you will be able to see how your fabric choices work together. If you are not satisfied with a fabric selection, peel off its freezer-paper template and iron the template on the back of another fabric. You will be able to re-iron the template several times.

Piecing

When some or all of the pieces have been cut, begin the sewing process. I use a 2.0 stitch length (12 stitches per inch) for piecing.

1. Begin with the straight seams. Put 2 pieces right sides together, matching the corners of the freezer-paper templates and the tick marks. Pin carefully so the pieces don't slip.

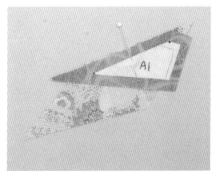

Match corners of freezer paper and ticks; pin.

2. Starting at the outside cut edge, sew the seam, using the edge of the freezer-paper templates as a guide all the way across to the other cut edge.

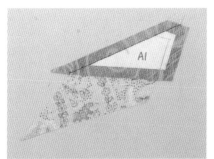

Sew along edge of freezer paper.

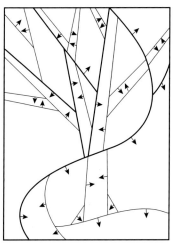

Press seams in direction of small arrows.

3. Press each seam in the direction of the small arrows. The seam allowances will pad the tree and make it stand out from the background when the piece is quilted. On the narrower pieces you may want to trim the seam allowances slightly after the seams have been sewn.

4. Sew the pieces in this order:

- A1 to A2 to A3
- B1 to B2 to B3 to B4 to A
- C1 to C2 to AB
- D1 to D2 to D3 to D4 to D5 to D6 to ABC
- E1 to E2 to E3 to E4 to ABCD
- F1 to F2 to F3
- G1 to G2 to G3; then G4 to G5 to G1G2G3

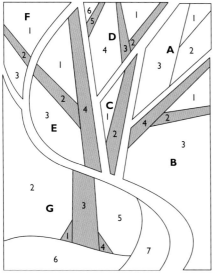

Assembly diagram. Sewing the block in sections

5. The remaining seams are all curved seams. Make sure you have marked the seamlines and ticks (as described above for curves, page 97) and clipped the concave edges. Remove the freezer-paper templates from all the pieces of fabric. Remember, you drew sewing lines on all those curves. You need to be able to manipulate the fabric to sew curves.

Tip

Always sew with the concave (clipped) piece on top.

6. Match G6 to G (1, 2, 3, 4, 5). Pin, matching the penciled seam allowances, the ticks, and the end corners and opening up the clips. Sew with G6 on the bottom. Press toward G6.

7. Join G7 to G (1, 2, 3, 4, 5, 6). Sew G to F.

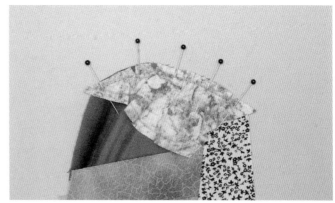

Sewing the curved seams, matching ticks

8. Match and pin FG to ABCDE from the center (☆) to the corner at the top (see the diagram for Step 3, page 97). Open the clips. Sew from the ☆ to the outside edge with FG on top. Remove from the machine.

9. Match and pin FG to ABCDE from the ☆ to the bottom corner. Open the clips. Overlapping the previous seam by a few stitches, sew, with FG on top, from the ☆ to the lower edge. Press the seam toward FG.

10. To use your small block for a little wall hanging, with the addition of a border as I have done with this one, cut 2 strips of border fabric $2^{1}/_{2}$″ × $10^{1}/_{4}$″ and sew them to the sides of the block, aligning the fabric and sewing along the edge of the paper. Cut 1 strip $2^{1}/_{2}$″ × $11^{3}/_{4}$″ and sew it to the top. Cut 1 strip $3^{1}/_{2}$″ × $11^{3}/_{4}$″ and sew it to the bottom.

11. Layer with batting and backing and quilt as desired. Trim the edges to square up the quilt.

You might also make your block into a pillow or a fabric book cover.

I've made a winter tree, but you could make a tree in spring, summer, or fall by using different foliage fabrics between the branches—or make all four blocks, one for each season, and sew them together for a larger project.

Cynthia England

Single template piecing works precisely and efficiently for a large and varied number of designs. It allows the easy piecing of patterns that would be difficult using traditional foundation pressed-piecing techniques. As with any technique, there is more than one way to proceed, and Cynthia England has created a very different way to use single templates. She first burst onto the scene in 1993 with *Piece and Quiet*, an extraordinary painterly quilt that uses more than 8,000 pieces of fabric!

Cynthia England is a graduate of the Art Institute of Houston and has been creating quilts for more than 30 years. She is an author, teacher, and lecturer, and her quilt *Piece and Quiet* was included in *The Twentieth Century's Best American Quilts*.

Picture piecing has the look of traditional foundation piecing, but it isn't the same. This is a freezer-paper technique that uses only straight lines and has no set-in seams. Seams are stitched next to the freezer paper, not through it.

Picture piecing uses several craft-related techniques.

- I make a color chart to organize the fabrics. This comes from crewel embroidery, in which threads are taped next to the numbers to organize the thread colors.

- The pattern uses the same breakout techniques that are used with stained glass, using a series of straight lines to create curves. When breaking up a picture-pieced design, I am doing basically the same thing with straight seams.

- In stained glass, as with appliqué, when you select pieces you can immediately see how one material appears in context with the others. In the picture-piecing technique, pattern pieces are pressed to the

PICTURE PIECING

My patterns look scary. They look scary to me and I create them. A cross-stitch pattern looks scary too, and it's only a bunch of little Xs. Think about the very first quilt you ever made. That seemed like an overwhelming project. Take a deep breath, learn the technique, and just go for it!

This snowbound cardinal is a great way to learn the picture-piecing technique. The pattern finishes as a 12″ block. It can be enlarged or reduced to any size. It would make a great medallion for the center of a quilt, or you could simply frame it or make a beautiful pillow.

Piece and Quiet (detail) by Cynthia England. See full quilt on page 125. Photo by Ken Wagner.

right side of the fabric so you can work with the shading and textures much more easily than in flip-and-sew foundation techniques.

The picture-piecing technique has definite advantages over other paper foundation techniques.

- There is less waste. I get confused when I foundation piece using pressed piecing. Either I flip too much fabric and waste fabric, or I don't have enough fabric. With picture piecing, you cut what you need.

- There is no picking out paper at the end. I don't like having to pick out paper from the seams even if I sewed them perfectly. You sew next to the paper, not through it.

- Picture piecing uses a standard stitch length. In pressed piecing, you must shorten the stitch length to make it easier to take the paper out later.

- What you see is what you get. The pattern pieces are ironed to the right side of the fabric, not the wrong side, so there is no mirror imaging and no guessing what to flip back. You can use the fabric to its best advantage.

- Picture piecing is fast. In picture piecing, you can chain piece. Any two pieces that match up can be sewn together.

- Pattern pieces can be reused.

Snowbound Cardinal

By Cynthia England

Quilt size: 16″ × 16″
Block size: 12″ × 12″

Materials

FABRIC

- Light blue background (B): ¼ yard
- Dark green tree (G2) and border: ¼ yard
- All other pieces: scraps of no more than ⅛ yard of each (I used tone-on-tone batiks, but you could easily use different shades of each color.)

Snowbound Cardinal. Learn how forgiving this technique can be as you make this striking red cardinal, created much like a puzzle.

You will use these colors:
G1 (tree): medium green; R1 (bird): medium red; R2 (bird): dark red; R3 (bird face): black; T (branch): brown; W (snow): white/gray; X (bird feet): tan; Y (bird beak): gold

- Backing: ⅝ yard
- Batting: 20″ × 20″
- Binding: ¼ yard

OTHER SUPPLIES

- Freezer paper for foundations
- Scissors (for cutting the small pieces)

Pattern preparation

One of the reasons the pattern looks so complicated is that each pattern piece has several pattern notations on it.

- *Circled numbers* identify pattern pieces.

- *Bold letters* and *bold lines* indicate major sections. These sections are sewn individually.

- *Dashed lines* indicate subsections.

- *Small letters* or *letters with numbers* show fabric colors.

- Generally seams do not have to align with other seams, but there are exceptions. Seams that need to match are indicated by a *circle over the intersection*.

1. Trace the pattern (on the pullout) on the dull side of freezer paper, using a pencil and a straightedge. Copy all lines and notations.

2. Make a photocopy of the master pattern as a reference for putting the pattern pieces back together.

3. Use a glue stick and make a color chart by cutting a small triangle of fabric for each color used in the quilt.

Preparing the foundations

1. Cut apart the freezer-paper pattern one section at a time on the heavy solid lines and then on the sub-section dotted lines. Sandwich bags are handy to keep the sections separated. During sewing, lay out the pattern pieces and work on one section at a time.

2. With the color chart as a guide, press the pattern pieces onto the right side of the corresponding fabrics. Use a cotton setting, no steam, and a hard ironing surface. I use a small travel iron during construction, keeping it right next to me. When the sections get large, I use my full-size iron.

3. When placing the pattern pieces on the right side of the fabric, leave ½" between each pattern piece. Because the width of your finger is about ½", place

Master diagram

your finger between 2 pattern pieces to gauge the proper distance for seam allowances.

4. Cut out leaving ¼″ around each pattern piece. Do not measure this—just eyeball it. Clip the corners of long, angular pieces. After 1 section of the pattern is ironed on and cut out, you are ready to sew.

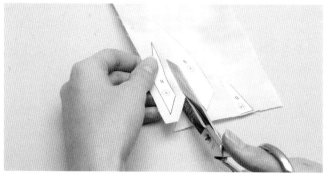

Cutting out pieces

Piecing

1. Work on 1 section at a time. Lay out the pattern pieces in a single layer on your sewing table. Use the circled numbers to identify the pieces as you prepare to sew them together. In other foundation piecing, pattern pieces must be sewn 1 at a time, in sequence. In picture piecing, you can sew any 2 that share a common seam. For instance, in section A, pattern pieces 1 and 2 can be sewn together as well as pieces 3 and 4, 7 and 8, and 14 and 15. Chain piece the pairs and continue to add to those. The larger the section, the more helpful it is to chain piece.

2. Place 2 pattern pieces that share a common seam right sides together. To align the pattern pieces, pull back 1 corner of the pattern piece on top and align the corners of the 2 freezer papers.

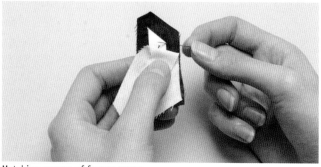

Matching corners of freezer paper

3. Pin the matched pieces in the center and use your fingers to fold the seam allowance back down along the freezer paper. This will give you a line to sew next to.

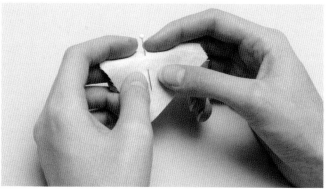

Pinning and pinching fold

4. Use a normal stitch length and sew slightly away from the fold. After sewing, the papers should be butted up next to each other. If they are not, do not rip the seam out—just peel off the freezer paper, realign the pattern pieces, and iron them in place where they should be.

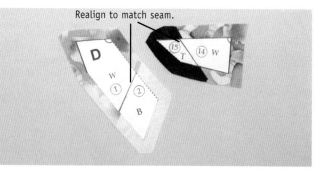

Realigning pattern pieces

Note: This is the best part of the whole technique. What is important is that the freezer papers align, not that the seam allowance falls exactly equally on each side. As long as the freezer paper templates are next to each other, the pattern will not go awry.

5. If a seam has to match, there is a circle over the intersection notation to remind you that this seam will align with another pattern piece.

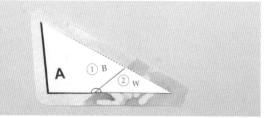

A circle at an intersection, signifying the need to match

6. Locate all the pieces within a section and stitch them first. Then continue to join pattern pieces until the section is completed. Chain stitch as much as you can in each section. The sections are sewn together just like the pairs: find two that are the same length and join them.

7. Detailed assembly instructions for the sections follow; however, once you get the hang of this technique you will not need them.

Section A: Sew 1 to 2, 3 to 4, 7 to 8, 14 to 15, 3–4 to 5, 7–8 to 9, 3–5 to 6, and 7–9 to 10, then 11, 12, and 13. Sew 3–6 to 7–13. Add 14–15. Add 1–2 to 3–15.

Section B: Sew 1 to 2, 4 to 5, 6 to 7, 14 to 15, 17 to 18, 21 to 22, and 24 to 25. Sew 1–2 to 3, 6–7 to 8, 14–15 to 16, and 17–18 to 19. Sew 1–3 to 4–5, then 6–8 to 9, 17–19 to 20, and 6–9 to 10, then 11, 12, and 13. Sew 1–5 to 6–13, then 14–16 to 17–20. Sew 1–13 to 14–20. Add 21–22, then 23, then 24–25 and 26.

Section C: Sew 1 to 2, 3 to 4, and 5 to 6. Sew 3–4 to 5–6 and add 7, then 8. Sew 1–2 to 3–8; add 9, then 10.

Section D: Sew 1 to 2, 3 to 4, 6 to 7, 8 to 9, and 10 to 11. Sew 1–2 to 3–4, and 6–7 to 8–9. Sew 1–4 to 5. Sew 1–5 to 6–9, then add 10–11.

Section E: Sew 1 to 2, 4 to 5, 6 to 7, 8 to 9, 11 to 12, 16 to 17, 19 to 20, 21 to 22, and 23 to 24. Sew 1–2 to 3, and 4–5 to 6–7, then add 8–9, then 10, then 11–12. Sew 1–3 to 4–12, then add 13, 14, and 15. Sew 16–17 to 18. Sew 1–15 to 16–18. Sew 19–20 to 21–22, and 23–24 to 25, then add 26, 27, 28, and then 29. Sew 19–22 to 23–29. Sew 1–18 to 19–29, then add 30.

Section F: Sew 1 to 2, and 3 to 4. Sew 3–4 to 5. Sew 1–2 to 3–5, then add 6, 7, and then 8.

Section G: Sew 1 to 2, 9 to 10, 12 to 13, 16 to 17, and 20 to 21. Sew 1–2 to 3, then 4, 5, 6, 7, and 8. Sew 9–10 to 11, and 12–13 to 14. Sew 16–17 to 18, and 20–21 to 22. Sew 9–11 to 12–14, and 16–18 to 19. Sew 1–8 to 9–14, then add 15. Sew 16–19 to 20–22. Sew 1–15 to 16–22.

Section H: Sew 1 to 2, 3 to 4, 7 to 8, and 9 to 10. Sew 3–4 to 5, then add 6. Sew 9–10 to 11, then add 7–8, then 12. Sew 1–2 to 3–6. Sew 1–6 to 7–12.

Section I: Sew 1 to 2, and 5 to 6. Sew 1–2 to 3, then add 4. Sew 5–6 to 7. Sew 1–4 to 5–7.

Section J: Sew 1 to 2, 5 to 6, 9 to 10, 11 to 12, 15 to 16, 20 to 21 and 22 to 23. Sew 1–2 to 3, 5–6 to 7, 11–12 to 13, and 15–16 to 17. Sew 1–3 to 4, 5–7 to 8, 11–13 to 14, and 15–17 to 18, then 19, then add 20–21. Sew 1–4 to 5–8, then add 9–10. Sew 1–10 to 11–14. Sew 1–14 to 15–21. Add 22–23.

Section K: Sew 1 to 2, 3 to 4, 13 to 14, and 16 to 17. Sew 3–4 to 5, then 6, 7, 8, 9, 10, 11, and 12. Sew 13–14 to 15, and 16–17 to 18. Sew 3–12 to 13–15, then add 1–2. Sew 1–15 to 16–18.

Section L: Sew 1 to 2, 4 to 5, 8 to 9, 11 to 12, and 14 to 15. Sew 1–2 to 3, and 4–5 to 6, then add 7. Sew 11–12 to 13. Sew 1–3 to 4–7, then add 8–9, then 10. Sew 11–13 to 14–15, then add 16. Sew 1–10 to 11–16.

Section M: Sew 1 to 2, and 4 to 5. Sew 1–2 to 3, and 4–5 to 6, then add 7. Sew 1–3 to 4–7.

8. Sew section A to B, C to D, E to F, G to H, J to K, and L to M. Sew AB to CD, and set aside. Sew GH to I, then add EF. Sew E–I to JK, then add LM. Sew A–D to E–M.

Troubleshooting Tips:

* Remember, if there is too much or too little space between the pattern pieces after you have sewn them, remove the freezer paper and realign.

* If you misplace a piece, simply trace another pattern piece onto freezer paper and iron it to fabric.

* If your stitching goes slightly onto the freezer paper, gently tug on both sides of the seam. Usually the paper will release itself. If not, remove the freezer paper and open the seam from the back to get any paper out.

* If the small pieces are giving you problems, try sewing 2 strips of fabric together. Iron the pattern pieces on the right side next to the seam, then cut them out as 1 piece.

* Another option: Sew a large scrap of fabric next to a larger pattern piece. Iron the small pattern piece on, then trim ¼″ around.

Sewing large scrap on before trimming to size

Finishing

1. Square up the block to 12½″. Cut 2 border strips 2½″ × 12½″ and sew to the top and bottom. Cut 2 strips 2½″ × 16½″ and sew to either side.

2. Layer with batting and backing and machine quilt, using clear monofilament thread on top and cotton thread in the bobbin. Outline the bird and some of the pine needles. You can also place batting behind the block and frame the piece instead of quilting it.

Caryl Bryer Fallert

One of the consummate quilters in the world is Caryl Bryer Fallert. Caryl was trained as an artist, and her landmark quilts have made a lasting impact on quiltmaking. Caryl has long worked with all the foundation techniques, and her newest application uses single templates and curves.

Caryl Bryer Fallert, of Paducah, Kentucky, is internationally recognized for her luminous, colorful, award-winning quilts, including *Corona 2: Solar Eclipse,* which was included in *The Twentieth Century's Best American Quilts*. Her attention to detail has earned her a reputation for fine craftsmanship as well as stunning designs with illusions of light, depth, and motion. She travels and teaches worldwide.

APPLIPIECING

When I began quilting in 1983, I made quilts with conventional squares, triangles, and blocks. Very quickly, I learned:

- Making a one-block quilt with lots of pieces is more fun than making the same block several times. Drawing the design more than once is tedious and often inaccurate.

- Multilayered compositions, with lots of visual interaction, are more interesting to me than random designs.

- Original works of art can be made using fabric as a medium.

- Appliqué is not fun for me.

- For me, curves are more fun than straight lines.

- If a seamline looks like it is supposed to line up and it doesn't, it distracts from the design and looks like a mistake.

- Misalignments can be seen and fixed ahead of time with a full-size drawing.

I began drawing my designs full-size on paper in 1984. By 1989 they had become so complex that piecing them conventionally (from the back with seams) became impossibly tedious and time-consuming. I began developing my applipiecing method in the summer of 1989 and it has been evolving ever since. By using one master drawing, which is cut up to make templates, I can be assured that everything will fit together perfectly. Even if I edit a bit with my scissors, the next template is automatically adjusted to make an exact fit. By joining the seams with invisible thread from the front, I can clearly see that everything is lined up. The 1mm × 1mm zigzag stitch is virtually invisible, barely perforates the

Garden Party (detail) by Caryl Bryer Fallert, see full quilt on page 126. Photo by Caryl Bryer Fallert.

edge of the paper, and doesn't interfere with removing the paper.

For me, applipiecing makes even the most convoluted designs possible, so I can focus on drawing the best designs possible. I am limited only by my imagination, not by wondering how I will piece the design together. The Square Dance block combines all the applipiecing tricks you need to know for even the most complicated patterns.

Square Dance

By Caryl Bryer Fallert

Quilt size: 22″ × 22″
Block size: 9″ × 9″

Pattern arrangement

If you plan to make a repeat-block quilt, experiment to find the arrangement you like the best. The square can be mirror imaged like a traditional quilt block. You can make 4 different symmetrical quilt blocks by placing each of the 4 corners in the center. You can also repeat the square in a pinwheel arrangement by rotating it from a corner. Now we have 8 different choices. Select the one you like best.

FABRIC

- 7 fabrics, in a variety of colors and values: $1/4$–$1/2$ yard of each, depending on their position in the blocks (See Cutting the Fabric, Steps 1–4, pages 108–109, for fabric suggestions.)
- Border: $3/8$ yard
- Backing: $3/4$ yard
- Batting: 26″ × 26″
- Binding: $1/4$ yard

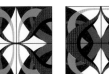

Possible arrangements of 4 blocks

With applipiecing, the colorful intertwining blocks of this wall quilt are fast, easy, and precise.

OTHER SUPPLIES

- Freezer paper
- Fine-point and ultra-fine-point felt-tip markers
- Clear and smoke-colored monofilament thread (polyester is recommended)
- Open-toe sewing machine foot
- #70/10 or smaller sewing machine needle
- Liquid or spray starch
- Cotton swab or watercolor brush
- Tape or glue stick
- Light box

Preparing the foundations

Tips for working with freezer paper

- Draw only on the dull/paper side of the freezer paper. Marks on the shiny side can be transferred to your fabric and may show through on lighter fabrics.

- When working with freezer-paper templates in this way, the block you make will always be a mirror image of the design you draw. The paper side is the wrong side, and the shiny right side is where the fabric will be.

● If you trace your pattern's seamlines with a marker, you will be able to see the lines on both sides. This will allow you to build your design shiny side up (fabric side) and see the fabric choices you have made. An ultra-fine-point marker is recommended for outlining the seamlines; use a fatter fine-point marker for the registration marks.

● Leaving the iron on the freezer paper for a long time can melt it into the fabric making it hard to remove. Iron just enough to make the fabric cling.

● If you change your mind about a fabric choice, the freezer paper can be peeled off and used on a second or third fabric.

Preparing the foundations

1. You will need to make registration marks across the curved lines dividing the templates to allow you to fit the templates back together perfectly after they are attached to the fabric. You will be folding a seam allowance over the edge of a template, so the line must be visible through 3 layers of fabric and a layer of freezer paper.

Making registration marks

2. The pattern has intersections where 2 sets of templates appear to cross. As soon as the templates are cut out, it will be hard to identify which line matches the seam and which line just matches another registration line. To help, these seamlines are marked with a V, which is an extended seamline with a little wing on it.

Intersection lines

3. A second kind of intersection, a "merge," is like getting on the freeway. There are 2 merges in the block. The edges of all the merging templates are perfectly smooth, so you need to mark the place where the long thin point of the center template intersects the other 2 templates on each side. If we put a V mark on each of the side templates, they will form an X straddling the line.

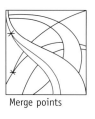

Merge points

4. Where there are obvious corners, registration marks are not necessary. These points are like crossroads, and when you are piecing these templates, you can simply line up the corners.

5. Trace the block (on the pullout) and all the registration marks on the dull side of the freezer paper with a fine-point marker. Transfer the numbers and letters, which are guidelines for fabric placement (numbers) and piecing order (letters).

6. Cut out the block on the outside line of the square. Do not add seam allowances. Carefully cut the templates apart along the seamlines. When cutting the templates with merging points, be sure to start your cut exactly at the X registration mark.

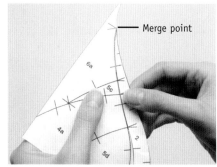

Merge point for shadow

Cutting the fabric

1. Begin with template 1. It will be the focal point of your block, so this is a good place to use your favorite fabric. Look for a pattern in the fabric that will complement the shape of the template. Lay template 1 shiny side down on the wrong side of the fabric and iron it in place. Cut the fabric approximately 1/4″ beyond the edge of the paper on all sides.

Template 1 on fabric

2. Template 2 is a shadow for template 1, so it will be cut from a solid black or other very dark fabric. Iron the template to the black fabric and cut it out just as you did with template 1, making sure you start or stop your cut exactly at the V mark.

3. Templates 3a and 3b will both be cut from the same fabric. Cut them out and iron both to the wrong side of a third fabric. Again, look for a pattern in the fabric that will complement the curved templates. Cut the fabric ¼″ from the edges of the paper as before.

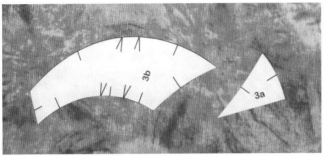

Templates 3a and 3b

4. Cut the remaining templates from fabrics 4–7 and arrange them together as they will be arranged in the finished block. The #5 templates will be cut from a fabric that is just slightly lighter than the #2 fabric, and the #6 templates will be cut from the lightest fabric. To create the illusion of transparency, select a color for template 7 that is slightly lighter than color 3 but not as light as color 6.

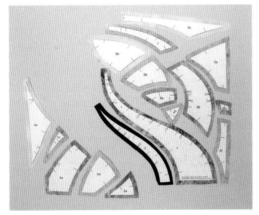

Templates arranged for sewing

Construction

In an applipiecing seam, one piece will have its seam allowance folded over the edge of the template, and the other piece will have the seam allowance lying flat. The 2 pieces will be slid together to make a perfect seam.

1. For the seam between templates 1 and 2, template 1 will be easier to fold. Long thin points like the one on template 2 are delicate and easy to distort, so leave them flat whenever possible. Template 1 has both a concave (inside) and convex (outside) curve.

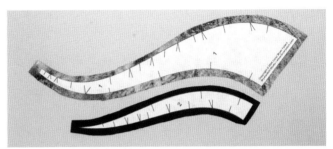

Templates 1 and 2 side by side

2. Seam allowances on some concave curves need to be clipped before they are folded over the edge of the paper. If the paper lifts up when you pull the seam allowance back over the edge of the paper, clip the seam allowance. Fold back the seam allowance over the paper and clip just to the edge of the paper.

The seam allowance on template 1 will be folded and clipped only as far as the V point where template 2 merges. We may want the rest of the seam allowance to lie flat—we will decide that when we are ready to join it to the next template.

3. Paint the seam allowance of template 1 with liquid starch up to the V where template 2 merges. Starting at the V, carefully fold the seam allowance over the edge of the freezer paper, ironing as you fold and easing in the extra fullness along the convex curve. The seam allowance from the V to the narrow end of template 1 will remain flat. Turn the template to the right side and make sure the folded edge is smooth.

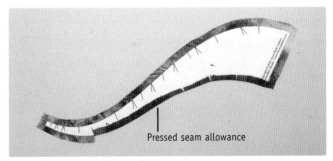

Pressed seam allowance

Seam allowance pressed up to the V

4. To line up the templates, follow these steps:

   a. Place templates 1 and 2 right side up on a light box.

   b. Lay the folded edge of template 1 over the flat seam allowance of template 2. Align the edges of the paper and all the registration marks, so the seam allowances are overlapped and the edges of the paper just butt together.

   c. Use pieces of cellophane tape or a glue stick along the folded seam allowance of template 1 to hold the edges in place. When using tape, cut the pieces about 2″ long and then fold over one end to make a handle. This will make it easier to remove the tape when you are sewing. Place the tape perpendicular to the seam.

Templates lined up, then taped

Stitching

1. Thread your sewing machine with monofilament thread. I recommend a small needle, a size 60/8 Microtex Sharp, to avoid making visible holes along the folded edge.

2. Set your machine stitch on zigzag, with a stitch length and width of 1mm. This is a very small stitch and will go right at the edge of the fold. By using an open-toe foot, you will be able to see exactly where the needle will go with each stitch.

3. Carefully stitch along the folded edge of template 1. When the needle swings toward template 1, it will just be catching 2–3 threads along the fold. When the needle swings toward template 2, it will clear the fold and only pierce the black fabric right next to the fold. If the needle pierces the fold on both swings of the needle, the stitching will show. When you stop or start stitching at the merging point of template 2, you may want to take a small backstitch. If you are using tape, remove it before sewing over it, as it is difficult to remove tape that has been stitched over with a zigzag.

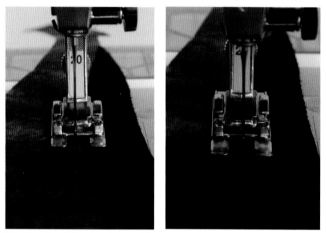

Stitching templates 1 and 2 together

Assembly

1. Assemble groups of templates into larger modules. For instance, 3a, 5d, 4a, 5c, and 6a can be joined in that order to make 1 piece. Folding the darker seam allowances will help avoid dark shadows under the lighter templates. If all 5 of the templates are taped or glued together first, you can save time by doing all the stitching at the same time. Remember to clip and fold just to the V where templates 4a and 5c merge.

2. Now we can join the new module to the module formed by templates 1 and 2. One module has 4 seams and one has 2 seams. Generally, we fold over the side with the least number of seams, but in this case we don't need to fold any seams. Clip to the straight registration mark on template 6a, and clip to the corresponding registration mark on template 2. Fold the seam allowance on template 6a from the registration mark to the outside point, and then fold the seam allowance on template 2 from the

registration mark to the wide end of the template. Remember to clip the concave curve on template 2. Use tape or a glue stick along the folded seam allowances on both modules.

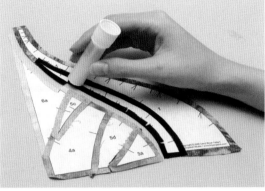

Preparing two modules, seams clipped and folded

3. On the light box, match up the clips at the common registration mark, and slide the folded seam allowances over the flat ones. Line up the remaining registration marks, tape or glue the pieces together, and begin stitching at 1 end of the seam.

4. When you reach the point where the 2 folded edges come together, lift the presser foot, shift over 1mm, and continue stitching on the other folded edge. The transition will be invisible.

5. Joining templates 6b, 5b, 4b, and 5e will form the next module. Joining 3b and 7 will form another, and joining 5f, 4c, 5a, and 6c will form yet another. Two long seams will join these 3 modules. Since the 3b and 7 module has only 1 seam, and the other has more, the seam allowance will be folded along both edges of that module.

6. Both of these seams have a crossroad where 2 seams cross. As you zigzag the pieces together, slow down and use a pin or a stiletto to adjust the seams so they match perfectly, and guide the matching point carefully under the needle.

You now have just 2 large modules to join before the block is complete. The edge of template 1 has no cross-seams, so that is the seam allowance we will fold. Carefully align the Vs on template 1 with the seams, stitch, and your block is complete. Press it carefully, straightening the edges if necessary and leaving a $1/4$″ seam allowance on all sides.

Finishing

1. Four blocks together will make a $18^1/_2$″ quilt top. Join the blocks by aligning the corners and stitching along the straight edge of the paper.

2. Cut 2 border strips $2^1/_2$″ × $18^1/_2$″ and 2 border strips $2^1/_2$″ × $22^1/_2$″. Adding a 2″ outer border will make the final wall hanging 22″ square. Attach the border by aligning the edges of the fabric and stitching along the straight edge of the paper.

3. Once the border has been attached, peel the freezer paper off the back of the templates. The stitching will barely perforate the edges of the templates if they were precisely aligned. If the paper seems hard to peel off, stretch the fabric on the bias and the paper will pop right out.

4. Layer with batting and backing and quilt, emphasizing the different design shapes.

Dixie Haywood
BLUE CRAZE

Lynn Graves
AUTUMN HARVEST

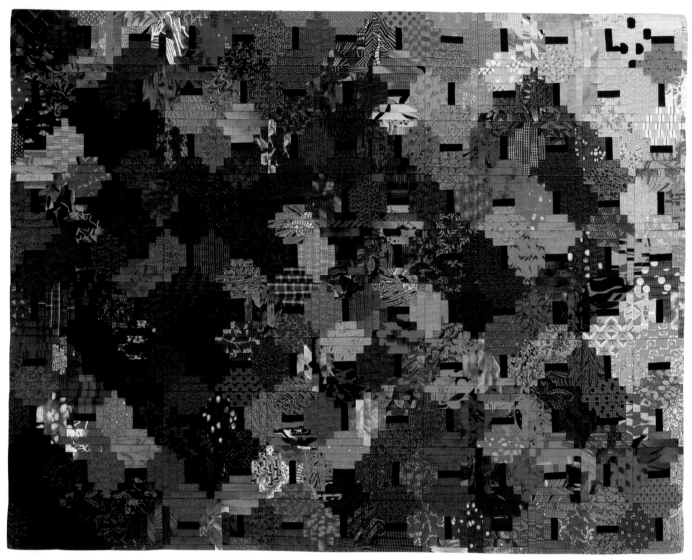

Lesly-Claire Greenberg
FLOWER DRUM SONG

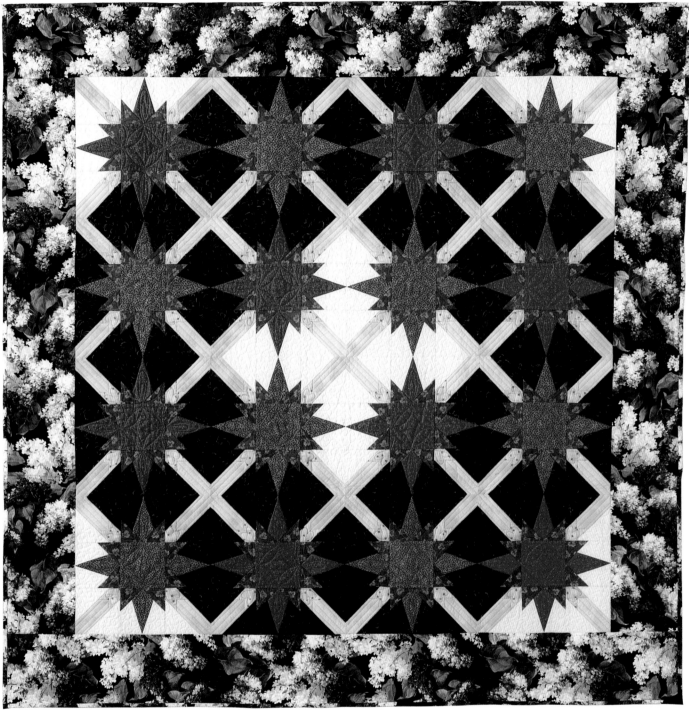

Carol Doak

STAR CROSSED

 *Jane Hall*

NEBULA

Barbara Barber
made by Keith Nuehring; Photo by Sharon Risedorph

OLD YELLER

Eileen Sullivan

WHEN GRANDMOTHER'S LILY GARDEN BLOOMS

Judy Mathieson
MARBLED STARS

Peggy Martin

NEW YORK BEAUTY

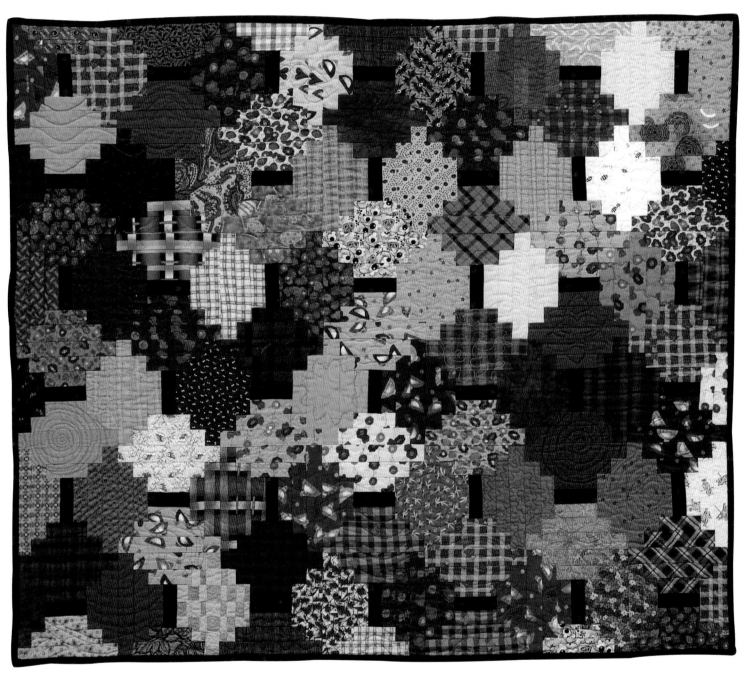

 *Anita Grossman Solomon*
SPENCER'S COURTHOUSE STEPS

Barb Vlack

IT'S CHIC TO BE SHABBY

Jane Hall
OP ART QUILT

 Ruth B. McDowell

LEAVES OF ANOTHER YEAR

Cynthia England
PIECE AND QUIET

Caryl Bryer Fallert

GARDEN PARTY

ABOUT THE AUTHOR

Jane Hall has been teaching and judging quiltmaking for quilt guilds and conferences for more than twenty years. Her particular love is foundation piecing, and she and her quilting partner, Dixie Haywood, have written several books exploring it.

Jane is intrigued by the interaction of colors and fabrics, and the graphics and geometry of quilt designs. She likes to work with traditional patterns, using innovative and contemporary colorations to create new graphics. She feels almost evangelistic about foundation piecing in all its forms, especially Log Cabin, Pineapple, and Mariner's Compass patterns.

Jane is a certified quilt teacher, judge, and appraiser. A graduate of Cornell University, she and her husband, Bob, have six grown children and twelve grandchildren. They live in Raleigh, North Carolina, with Tilly, the calico cat.

RESOURCES

MARCI BAKER
1031 Conifer Street, #6
Ft. Collins, CO 80524
www.aliciasattic.com
Teacher, author; patterns, "Know-Before-You-Sew" solution cards including E.F.P.E. (Everyone Foundation Pieces Easily).

*BARBARA BARBER
Ramridge Dene, Ramridge Park
Weyhill, Andover
Hants, SP11 OQP England
Teacher, author, designer.

CM Designs
Carolyn McCormick
7968 Kelty Trail
Franktown, CO 80116
Add-a-Quarter and Add-an-Eighth rulers, made especially for trimming foundation piecing.

*CAROL DOAK
PO Box 42
Windham, NH 03087
www.caroldoak.com
Teacher, author of several foundation-piecing books and patterns, Foundation Factory CDs, Carol Doak's Foundation Paper.

*CYNTHIA ENGLAND
England Design
1201 Sunset Drive
Dickinson, TX 77539
www.englanddesign.com
Teacher, author, original patterns, hard-to-find fabrics, and quilt tools.

The Electric Quilt Company
419 Gould Street, Suite 2
Bowling Green, OH 43402
www.electricquilt.com
Quilt design software, books, foundation sheets and printable fabric sheets.

*CARYL BRYER FALLERT
Bryerpatch Studio
PO Box 116
Paducah, KY 42002
www.bryerpatch.com
Teacher, author; hand-dyed fabrics in color gradations, original patterns, art quilts.

Graphic Impressions
1090 Highpoint Drive
Nicholasville, KY 40356
Easy-Tear™ lightweight removable interfacing, stencils, patterns.

*LYNN GRAVES
Little Foot, Ltd.
PO Box 1027
Chama, NM 87520
www.littlefoot.net
Teacher, author; patterns, quilting notions including Little Foot® for $1/4$" seams, and Big Foot® for free-motion quilting.

*LESLY-CLAIRE GREENBERG
Quilt Arts
4114 Minstrell Lane
Fairfax, VA 22033
Teacher, author, pattern designer.

*DIXIE HAYWOOD
127 Canterbury Road
Pendleton, SC 29670
Teacher, author of several foundation and crazy-piecing books, quilt judge.

*PEGGY MARTIN
13415 Sawtooth Road
San Diego, CA 92129
www.peggymartinquilts.com
Teacher, author of several strip-piecing books.

*JUDY MATHIESON
1977 Green Hill Road
Sebastopol, CA 95472
www.judymathieson.com
Teacher, author of several Mariner's Compass books, quilt judge.

*RUTH B. MCDOWELL
993 Main Street
Winchester, MA 01890
www.ruthbmcdowell.com
Teacher, author of several design and piecing books, original patterns, art quilts.

*ANITA GROSSMAN SOLOMON
444 East 57th Street, #13F
New York, NY 10022
www.MakeItSimpler.com
Teacher, author of several foundation-piecing books, Simple Foundations vellum paper.

*EILEEN SULLIVAN
The Designer's Workshop
PO Box 1026
Duluth, GA 30096
www.thedesignersworkshop.com
Teacher, author; patterns for original foundation designs, die-cut freezer paper.

*BARB VLACK
36 W. 556 Wild Rose Road
St. Charles, IL 60174
Teacher, author of several computer books, designer with The Electric Quilt Company.

Zippy Designs
RR1, Box 187M
Newport, VA 24128
www.quiltswithstyle.com
Quilts with Style magazine (formerly *The Foundation Piecer*), books, patterns, notions, Easy Piece foundation paper.

*contributors to *The Experts' Guide to Foundation Piecing*

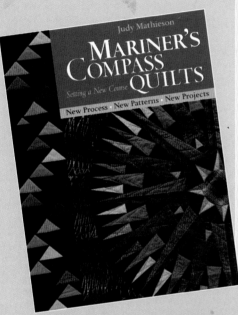
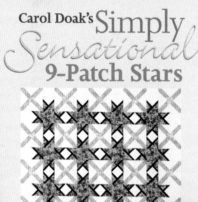

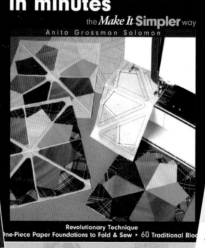